The Spark,
the Flame,
and the
TORCH

Other Books by Lance Secretan
ONE: *The Art and Practice of Conscious Leadership*
Inspire! What Great Leaders Do
Spirit@Work: Bringing Spirit and Values to Work
Inspirational Leadership: Destiny, Calling and Cause
Reclaiming Higher Ground: Creating Organizations
That Inspire the Soul
Living the Moment: A Sacred Journey
The Way of the Tiger: Gentle Wisdom for Turbulent Times
The Masterclass: Modern Fables for Working and Living
Managerial Moxie: The 8 Proven Steps to Empowering Employees
and Supercharging Your Company

CDs by Lance Secretan
ONE: *The Art and Practice of Conscious Leadership: An Intensive*
7-Day Audio Retreat
Inspire! What Great Leaders Do
Inspirational Leadership: Destiny, Calling and Cause
Reclaiming Higher Ground: Creating Organizations
That Inspire the Soul
Living the Moment: A Sacred Journey
The Keys to the CASTLE: The Magic of Higher Ground Leadership
The New Story of Leadership: Reclaiming Higher Ground
Values-centered Leadership: A Model for Work and Life
The Calling Meditation

Videos and DVDs by Lance Secretan
DreamQuest: The Journey to Higher Ground DVD Series
Inspire! What Great Leaders Do
Inspirational Leadership: Destiny, Calling and Cause
Reclaiming Higher Ground: Creating Organizations That
Inspire the Soul
The Keys to the CASTLE: The Magic of Higher Ground Leadership
Values-centered Leadership: A Model for Work and Life

The Spark, the Flame, and the TORCH

LANCE H. K. SECRETAN

*Twelve Reflections that will help you discover a
fresh sense of personal awareness, values, and
meaning, leading to heightened personal inspiration
and ability to inspire and lead others*

THE SECRETAN CENTER INC.

Library of Congress Cataloging in Publication Data

Secretan, Lance H. K.
    The spark, the flame, and the torch : inspire self, inspire others, inspire the world / Lance H.K. Secretan.

Includes index.

ISBN 978-0-9865654-0-3

1. Leadership. 2. Organizational effectiveness. I. Title.

HD57.7.S434 2010   658.4'092   C2010-902010-3

Published by The Secretan Center Inc.
Caledon, Ontario, Canada

Cover design: Cattails Multimedia
Text design: Heidy Lawrance, Heidy Lawrance Associates
Printed in Canada

The following terms, appearing in this book, are registered or applied for trademarks of The Secretan Center Inc.:
Higher Ground Leadership®
Inspirational Leadership®
Values-centered Leadership®
ONE Dream™
CASTLE™ and The CASTLE™ Principles

If you would like to contact the author to order his books, videos, DVDs, or CDs, or to arrange a public speaking engagement, please do so at the following coordinates:

Dr. Lance H. K. Secretan
The Secretan Center Inc.
(519) 927-5213

www.secretan.com
E-mail: info@secretan.com

Second printing

Dedicated to all the wonderful people who have shared their inspiring stories with me, and which I have, in turn, shared in this book, including that of Oberleutnant L. Franz Stigler and Lieutenant Charles Brown, whose remarkable tale exemplifies the love and inspiration that we are all yearning for in each other. We desire to travel, as they all did, the hero's journey.

Life is no brief candle to me. It is a sort of splendid torch which I have got a hold of for the moment, and I want to make it burn as brightly as possible before handing it on to future generations.

George Bernard Shaw

Table of Contents

ACKNOWLEDGMENTS

In the age of e-book readers and turbulence in the world of physical books, there is one constant: to successfully complete the momentous task of writing and publishing a book, an author needs many friends and helpers. A fellow author recently told me that writing a book was as close as I would ever get to experiencing pregnancy and childbirth. I am not sure if this is true, but I get the point. It takes a caring, passionate, brilliant team to create a book, and I am fortunate and grateful for the many committed individuals who have guided this project, delivering the end result smoothly into your hands—whether it is real or virtual.

Thanks to Simone Gabbay, who has been kneading my prose for many years, in many languages, and with many books—she is a true professional and much more than an editor.

The team at The Secretan Center Inc. has supported and nurtured me during the arduous phases of development and research, especially Tricia Field, Tracey Gilmore, Ken Jacobsen, Ron Mandel, Al Moscardelli, and Julie Snyder.

Thanks to the brilliant teams at 5 Dynamics: Karen Gordon, Mike Sturm, Melissa Wells, and David Zweig; and at Scientific Intelligence: Penelope Fridman, Jacob Kessler, Syd Kessler, and Wahn Yoon.

The Spark, the Flame, and the Torch describes ideas that have been developed with clients and then successfully implemented in their organizations. Our clients not only provided the wherewithal that supported the time-consuming writing phases of this book (which took over four years to complete), but also the laboratory in which to experiment and apply new (and sometimes radical and challenging) ideas. Their feedback has been invaluable in guiding the evolution and fine-tuning of many of the concepts you will read about in this book. I am especially grateful to Deb Gmelin, Bonnie Hathcock, Paul Kusserow, Mike McCallister, Tom Noland, Raja Rajamannar, Chris Todoroff, and Ray Vigil of Humana Inc., and Marty Durbin, Scott Spiker, and Mike Wheeler of First Command Financial Services, where amazing work has been done in partnership with each of them over several years and incomparable feedback received. Thanks also to Marc Benioff, Nolan Berg, Sue Carruthers, Len Crispino, Sister Nancy Hoffman, Dave Mowat, Joe Reagan, Rob Ryder, Tracee Troutt, and Shirley Willihnganz.

I am also deeply grateful to my inspiring community of friends in skiing. From them I have learned so much, and the metaphors in snow sports are so rich and plentiful. Phil Anderson, JP Chevalier, Don Coleman, Trish and Moe Dixon, Ari Goosen, Stephen "Karpy" Karp, Lyle Knudsen, Joe Rota, and Jeff "Stumpy" Stump have all helped me to raise the quality of my skiing at an age at which most other people are settling into their comfort zone. Participants in our Leadership Summits in the ski hills lived the breakthroughs on the mountain and then took them back to their homes and work. And Alexa Loo, Bode Miller, Lindsey Vonn, and Shaun White fired my imagination by demonstrating the power of having a dream, obliterating old limitations, and raising the bar for all who follow.

It is a blessing when one's agent is also one's friend, and Ron Szymanski of the Leigh Bureau epitomizes this gift.

A Community of Torchbearers and Secretan Associates and supporters has grown while we have been developing this project, and their encouragement has been enormously helpful. Among them are: Wally Amos, James Bond, Ed Boudreau, Erika Caspersen, Garry Cuff, Leo Deveau, Dr. John Green, Rob Grundison, Tom Heck, Randy Judge, Larry Lambert, Shonnie Lavender, Adrian Legin, David Long, Rick Mavrovich, Laura

McCafferty, Francisco Moisés, Robin Mooney, Scott Regan, Nancy Ward, Steve Robinson, Elizabeth Skronski, Stu Zimmerman, and Don Ziraldo.

Thanks to Heidy Lawrance and her team at Heidy Lawrance Associates, the shepherds of the design process, and Fred Cheetham of Friesens, who, once again, have offered incomparable printing and production services, and to the team at Cattails Multimedia, who translate the ideas presented in this book into magical multimedia shows. They also designed the cover for this book.

Titling a book is a maze with many cul-de-sacs and one or two eurekas. Frank Costantini, brilliant creative guru at ON Ideas, helped me think through the subtitle of this book, while my wife, Tricia, and I developed the main title during one of our hikes on the Colorado Trail.

Tricia, of course, is my cherished life partner, and I am immensely grateful to her for the constant love, support, inspiration, and understanding she offered during the many months that I spent more time with *The Spark, the Flame, and the Torch* than I did with her. We are ONE, Tricia!

PREFACE

We are emerging from a dark era of leadership. According to the Conference Board, between 1987 and 2009, the level of employee job satisfaction plummeted from 61 percent to 45 percent, and the number who find their work interesting sank from 70 percent to 51 percent. Equally disturbing, the greatest levels of dissatisfaction are among those under the age of twenty-five—our most precious source of tomorrow's leaders. According to Rasmussen Reports, 45 percent of likely voters in the United States think a group of people selected at random from the phone book would do a better job of leading America than the current Congress. The leadership style that gave us the Great Recession is not the leadership style that can build a resilient and inspiring future.

People are hurting—financially, spiritually, emotionally, and physically. We are leaving what *Time* magazine called "The Decade from Hell," and there is a yearning for a new beginning, an opportunity to create and enjoy a brighter future—a Decade of Meaning and Fulfillment.

There is a growing movement that seeks to restore joy, significance, and personal worth in work and life. It is a movement formed by leaders who are leaving old ideas of leadership behind and adopting new philosophies that inspire others to get things done and to live meaningful and fulfilling lives.

Why do some people seem to have an aura about them, a presence, an ability to inspire others that gets things done and enables them to live meaningful and fulfilled lives? What makes them special, extraordinary, happy, and a delight to be around? Since we have all the information, tools, and skills necessary to live an inspired life, why don't we all live and lead in this way?

This book seeks to answer those questions.

The Spark Ignites the Flame, and the Flame Lights the Torch

In Part One, we will explore the concept of the "Spark"—the initial energy that kindles the embers of inspiration within each of us, that moves us to live large and to inspire others, to reach our highest potential, to make a meaningful difference in our own life, the lives of others, and the world. Without the spark, we are ordinary and dull, and we aim below our promise. This dullness is the absence of passion and energy, of dreams and magic in our lives, of relationships that inspire, and of bearings that lead to meaning and fulfillment, excitement, and zest. The spark initiates fusion, combustion, and reaction. The spark is awakened by a newly realized, deep inner awareness of **Why** we are here on Earth, how we will **Be** while we are here, and what we have been called upon to **Do**. Few people have discovered the answers to these questions, or have even cared to explore them. They are content to live the unexamined life—and as Socrates said, "The unexamined life is not worth living." On the other hand, those who have reflected thoughtfully on these questions, and defined the right answers for themselves, have ignited the spark within them. This is the often-silenced voice of the soul, and this we call the *Why-Be-Do*—**Why** we are here, how we will **Be**, and what we will **Do**. When you stand in the presence of someone who has a deep, inner knowing of who they are—an awareness of **Why** they are here on Earth, how they will **Be** while they are here, and what they have been called to **Do**—you are standing in the presence of an inspiring person. This is the "spark" that flashes and radiates from within them. Their certainty about their path, and the passion they have for it, makes them the kind of person that others want to be with and to follow, firing up their own hopes for living the same way.

This inner awareness creates a fusion with their higher purpose and causes a powerful release of energy. It causes them to be inspiring—they can't help themselves, because it radiates from within them and stirs the hearts of others.

The spark ignites the flame. In Part Two, we will explore the "Flame"—the fire within us that lights the way for others, that generates intensity and raises the temperature, that fires the spiritual and emotional rockets of our lives, that takes us to unexplored places of promise. The flame is bright and visible to all—it represents the values we practice and passionately believe in and model for others. The flame fuels a fervor that informs all our actions and illuminates the path for others. It is our standard against which we calibrate our conduct. It represents the behaviors we model for others and teach to them, and which, in turn, encourage them to ignite their own spark and add their own fire to their flame. The flame is a set of values we call the CASTLE Principles— "CASTLE" being an acronym for six inspiring ways of being:

- *Courage*: Reaching beyond the boundaries of our existing limitations, fears, and beliefs
- *Authenticity*: Being genuine, transparent, and aligned with our inner voice in all aspects of life
- *Service*: Willing, and actively supporting, the good of the other
- *Truthfulness*: Being honest and transparent in all thoughts, words, and actions
- *Love*: Relating to others by touching their hearts in ways that add to who we both are as persons
- *Effectiveness*: Achieving desired outcomes successfully

As we live by these principles, we are the flame by which others are warmed, guided, developed, comforted, and inspired. This is how we change the world.

The flame lights the torch. In the final section of the book, we will discuss the "Torch"—the legacy we create and the wisdom we pass on, the gift of mentoring, coaching, and contributing to the growth of others—how we convert the spark into a flame, using it to light the torch, which we share with others. The flame is used to light the torch, and the torch is used to carry fire to others. The torch is "paying it forward," teaching others, helping them to grow, and being an inspiring mentor for them. It is with our torch that we light the way for others. As Carl Jung reminded us, "As far as we can discern, the sole purpose of human existence is to kindle a light in the darkness of mere being."

To live the inspired and inspiring life, we pass through these three progressions: We become inspired: *the Spark*; We live an inspiring life: *the Flame*; and, We share with others the opportunity to do the same: *the Torch*.

In Part One, you will be guided through interactive exercises that enable you to ignite your spark by discovering and crafting your own statements of why you are here in the world, how you want to be while you are here, and how you will use your gifts and talents to serve; in Part Two, you will gain insights into how you will light your flame by committing to how you will live your life; and, lastly, in Part Three, we will discuss ways to pass the torch by becoming an inspiring person who serves, leads, inspires, and contributes to the growth of others.

INTRODUCTION

> Don't ask yourself what the world needs; ask yourself what
> makes you come alive. And then go and do that. Because what
> the world needs is people who have come alive.
>
> Harold Whitman

In 2007, John Paulson had the largest personal payday in Wall Street history—$3.7 billion (yes, *billion*!). To put that in perspective, this was about $10 million a day, and it was more than the combined earnings of J.K. Rowling, Oprah Winfrey, and Tiger Woods for that year, more than the gross domestic product of 36 countries, or one out of five of all the economies in the world. He made this one-year, outsize fortune betting against financial institutions who were lending money to homeowners who had, at best, only a marginal ability to repay their mortgages. When the "subprime crisis" occurred, banks and financial institutions veered towards a default cliff, writing off more than $300 billion in losses, while one of the venerable top five banks in America, Bear Stearns, collapsed, along with the United Kingdom's Northern Rock and many other financial institutions around the world, and Americans ended up owing more in mortgages than all the real estate being financed by them, deflating the American housing market and triggering recessions in numerous countries.

There is no judgment implied here—it is just a vivid example of the inspirational void in which we find ourselves. Whenever we pursue financial rewards alone, it leads to an imbalance that causes a personal and collective dysfunction. Our social and corporate cultures have developed into ones that brilliantly reward the metrics of performance while overlooking the measures of the heart, and this has caused an evaporation of inspiration. Leaders today are remunerated on the basis of a set of performance metrics that measure material progress, but not spiritual or human fulfillment. We measure and reward improvements in share price, return on capital, market share, market capitalization, shareholder return, larger budgets, and so forth, but not meaning, fulfillment, inspiration, joy, or improvements in the human condition or the health of the planet. In other words, we measure and reward the external, but not the internal. And emphasizing the external alone can give us a false sense of happiness—our true joy comes from the internal.

Compared to our conventional metrics, there are no equivalent ones for inspiring and serving customers,[1] creating a loyal and devoted workforce, nurturing their spirit, being kind and sensitive to the environment, honoring our communities and the people who live in them, being caring supporters of the disadvantaged, making the necessary trade-offs and sacrifices and taking the risks that make the world better, or living to more than "the-minimum-required-by-law" standards of ethics, morals, and values. Even when we do pay attention to these matters, our measurement tools are often poorly calibrated. We reward the creation of wealth, but not stewardship—the outer, but not the inner. And there is a natural law that governs all this: we get the results we reward.

---

[1] Please, let's stop calling human beings "consumers." The term "consumer" is demeaning and inaccurate, and it separates me from you instead of seeking to make me one with you. I am a person. Please refer to me as a person, and when there are several of us, refer to us as people—and if you must use business jargon, then honor me as a customer or a client.

And, perhaps most importantly, we have forgotten how taking care of each other and our planet is the pinnacle of inspiring behavior—for both those who care and those who are cared for. Indeed the most effective metric for measuring how well we serve the spirit is the degree to which others find each of us inspiring—as people or organizations.

Meanwhile, the paradox is that as the baby boomers ease into retirement, the next generation is demanding more meaning, fulfillment, compassion, and engagement, causing leaders to scramble as they search for relevant new approaches, even as they try to rework centuries-old leadership tools, theories, beliefs, and practices. For leaders today, there seem to be more questions than answers—What is important? What is of value? What adds value? Where do people fit in? What should we trade off? How do we inspire the soul? Is there more than making the numbers each quarter?

These are the questions asked by leaders facing a crisis of inspiration.

These are the questions that this book will seek to answer. And if this book succeeds in igniting a spark within you, then a new flame will begin to burn—*and your life will change.*

The degree to which each of us is inspiring is determined by the degree to which each of us is inspired ourselves. Uninspired people cannot inspire others—it isn't within them. In fact, no one can inspire another person unless they are themselves inspired—parent, CEO, minister, firefighter, politician, rock star, author—no one. *We experience the world not as it is, but as we are.* Inspired people, therefore, cannot help themselves from inspiring others—it radiates from within them and affects everyone around them, because that is who they are.

Those of you who are familiar with my work will notice that the themes introduced here are consistent with a philosophy I have been developing over many years. While I have advanced many theories over the last 30 years, some of which have been recorded in my earlier books, I consider this to be a "master-work" because, for the first time, I have integrated all of these ideas into a seamless "grand theory" of how to inspire people, organizations, and the world. I have learned a great deal from the leaders with whom I have worked and partnered over the last four decades, and as I formulate and articulate my thinking and they then put it into practice in their organizations and lives, the applied theories sometimes work differently from their abstract beginnings. As a result of the kind advice and shared experiences of many clients, some of my earlier concepts have been funda-mentally reworked, while others have merely been tweaked. Since we are all growing—or should be—ideas deemed so relevant and smart yesterday may seem like candidates for revision today. Astronomies change, but the stars are perpetual. I have been especially struck by the intense and growing need of the leaders I know, for something they can believe in, something that demands and engages their deepest passion. These leaders seek to ensure that their lives are fueled by passion, have meaning, and that they are needed in the world. This passion-fueled desire and awareness are the source of their own inspiration and they cre-ate the energy that inspires those they lead. Opportunity may only knock once, but passion leans on the doorbell.

It's Not Just About "Leadership"

I have spent many years as a practicing leader, including 14 years with a *Fortune 200* company. I have written 15 books about leadership, taught the subject at universities, and coached many leaders worldwide, and along the way, I have come to the con-clusion that "leadership," as a discipline or activity, may simply be a subset of something larger—the practice of being an inspir-ing individual. It is *inspiration* that leads to progress; gets things done; shifts opinions, ideas, and beliefs; creates organizations and grows people; and changes the world. While the process and styles of leadership are important topics, they are far less important than the art of inspiring others. All great leaders are inspiring—but so are great mothers and fathers, siblings, friends, colleagues, and employees. Inspiration depends on a relationship —inspiration cannot occur unless one human being touches the heart of another. Thus leadership in its rather dry, detached, academic form, as we have come to know it—"old-story" leadership—may run the risk of being uninspiring, especially when it is imperial, mechanical, or theoretical. As Stanford University emeritus professor James G. March puts it, "Leadership involves plumbing as well as poetry," and, using a similar construction allegory, Colleen C. Barrett, former CEO of Southwest Airlines, said, "When it comes to getting things done, we need fewer architects and more bricklayers." So the philosophical concept that underpins this book is that if we first become more inspiring as people, we are then able to become inspiring leaders—or inspiring pianists, athletes, or bus drivers, or any other vocation or social role we choose. It's not really just about leadership—it's about being inspirational—which is a necessary condition of greatness in all other things.

Beginning a Movement

We could take this idea further. Suppose that you and I make a decision that the very first thing we do each day is to make a commitment that all our thoughts, communications, and actions will be inspiring. If we make this simple pledge and then follow through on our intention, our impact on those around us will be remarkable and we will change our lives—and theirs. And if a million people took this pledge, we would change the world. Are you prepared to make this commitment? And are you prepared to take action by enrolling your friends and colleagues in this simple endeavor? With your help, support, encouragement, and passion, this can become a *movement*.[2]

---

[2] See p. 219, and please sign the Inspire Pledge at www.secretan.com/inspirepledge

Try it: as you begin your day, repeat the mantra, "Inspire." The word "inspire" is from the Latin *spirare*, which means *to breathe*. Breathe in the word "Inspire" and take it fully into your entire body. Circulate the energy of Inspiration through your heart, pumping the life force of Inspiration through your circulatory system to all your organs and every part of your body. Make a commitment to *be* that word for the rest of the day. Say to yourself, "Inspire! I pledge to be an inspiring person in every thought, word, and deed." Breathe in the awareness of Inspiration every chance you get; after all, it's always only a breath away. As you put this declaration into practice, the world will become richer for having experienced you. This is how you can make the difference that you, like all of us, yearn for. The word "conspire" means to breathe together (con=with; spirare=to breathe); let's breathe together—let's conspire to change the world and make our experience of being alive more inspiring.

Another theme of this book is the pursuit of elegance woven with simplicity. In many disciplines, including management and leadership, we tend to complicate things too much. The art of explaining complex ideas by distilling them into very simple applications is at the heart of the messages I wish to convey here.

My wish for you is that this book will help you to reinvent the way you think about how you relate to others and the world—how inspiring you are. My intention is to be there with you through our dialogue and the exercises designed to help you to reinvigorate your life, redefine your dreams, and infuse new passion into your very existence.

Lao-Tzu said, "It is wisdom to know others; it is enlightenment to know one's self." By reflecting on the concepts presented here, you will be able to redefine the passion within you and how it inspires your life. It will take some effort—some reading, some reflection, and some meditation. But if you invest in and sustain the necessary energy to work through the twelve chapters (or, as I have called them, *Reflections*), you will discover the *real* reason why you have been put on Earth, what you have been called to do while you are here, how you will do it, how you will serve, how you will invite others to fully participate with you, and how you can become more inspired yourself and therefore be an inspiration to others.

In this book, you will notice frequent references to Higher Ground Leadership®. This is a collective name we have given to a breakthrough leadership philosophy that questions, deepens, and enriches conventional thinking (the "old story") with a new wisdom based on teachings that have been adapted to our modern needs (the "New Story"). Practitioners of this philosophy are known as Higher Ground Leaders, and one of their characteristics is their clear inner knowing about who they are. As we stated earlier, when you stand in the presence of someone who has a deep, inner knowing of who they are, someone who is very clear about **Why** they are here on Earth, how they will **Be** while they are here, and what they have been called to **Do** (the *Why-Be-Do*), you are standing in the presence of an inspiring person—the inspiration radiates from within them. They are certain about their path and have a powerful passion for it, and this makes them the kind of person that others want to be with and follow—the kind of person others find inspiring.

This leads to a way of being that is the result of a series of sacred insights, and clarifying those insights comprises the first five Reflections in this book. How to live in a way that always inspires others, and therefore ourselves, is described in the next six Reflections. And how we "pay it forward"[3] is described in the final Reflection.

Being clear about who we are, living to a set of affirming values, and helping others to grow requires us to be inclusive—to honor the sacredness of others—regardless of their beliefs or

---

[3] The expression "to pay it forward" describes the concept of generalized reciprocity, in which the recipient of a good deed or favor does a favor to a third party instead of returning the favor.

faith. In addition to the distinction between religion and spiritu-
ality that is woven throughout this book, the notion of *inclusion*
is equally important. As Garrison Keillor said, "Going to church
no more makes you a Christian than sleeping in your garage
makes you a car." And Gandhi said with less wit but more elegance, "There are no religions in Heaven." I seek not to offend
anyone, but rather to *include* everyone, as the God I believe in
has counseled me to do. Everything is connected—as Francis
Thompson wrote:

> *All things by immortal power,*
> *Near and Far*
> *Hiddenly*
> *To each other linked are,*
> *That thou canst not stir a flower*
> *Without troubling of a star.*

We cannot be inspiring or inspire others if we exclude them,
or disconnect from the whole, and we are most inspiring when
we incorporate a connection to a higher presence in ourselves,
our work, and our aspirations—honoring the sacredness of
everyone. We inspire others when we reduce the circle of those
we exclude and widen the circle of those we include—until there
is only one circle. As Howard Winters remarked, "Civilization is
the process in which one gradually increases the number of people included in the term 'we' or 'us' and at the same time
decreases those labeled 'you' or 'them' until that category has no
one left in it." Inspiring others requires that we include them, not
exclude them. As Edwin Markham wrote,

> *He drew a circle that shut me out;*
> *Heretic, rebel, a thing to flout.*
> *But love and I had the wit to win:*
> *We drew a circle that took him in.*

The aim of this book is ambitious: to help you gain a new and deeper insight into your life and the inspiring role you were born to play, and by so doing, help you to transform the organization you lead, or work within, into one that inspires you and everyone else more, and to be an inspiration in all other aspects of your life, too—for work and life are not separate, either. This book will guide you to work from the inside out rather than the outside in—the opposite to the underpinnings of almost all contemporary leadership theory.

The Art of Peace begins with you. Work on yourself and your appointed task in the Art of Peace. Everyone has a spirit that can be refined, a body that can be trained in some manner, a suitable path to follow. You are here for no other purpose than to realize your inner divinity and manifest your innate enlightenment. Foster peace in your own life and then apply the Art to all that you encounter.

Morihei Ueshiba

PART ONE

THE SPARK
Why Are You Here?

Passion and inspiration cannot appear without the prior ignition of a spark. The spark is essential for all of us to be inspired—it fires up the will. A spark must be present in order to initiate excitement, passion, a hunger of the spirit, an ambition to accomplish something special, to make a difference. The spark is a sudden awareness, a stirring within, an awakening of our potential, a growing enthusiasm, a realization that we can live large and are capable of changing the world. Without the spark, we are plodding and boring, and our aspirations—both for ourselves and for others—will lack the spiritual oxygen that fuels a flame. This is the listless life that seeps out into the world from us to others, and it is uninspiring—to us and to others, too. The spark ignites the soul. Thomas Merton said, "Our real journey in life is interior: it is about growth, deepening, and a constant surrender to the deeds of love and grace. This is your calling, and it will bring only joy." The spark arouses the desire to make a difference, to inspire people, adding electricity, brio, and zest—the stuff that fans the flames of passion and exhilaration within others and brings joy to all. When we have the spark, others feel their lives to be larger, they become more fulfilled, and they feel richer for having experienced us in their lives. This is how the world becomes changed.

SETTING OUR INTENTIONS

Life begets life. Energy creates energy. It is by spending oneself that one becomes rich.

Sarah Bernhardt

A little-appreciated reality is that the majority of people are aching to make a commitment in their lives—to others, to a goal, to the world—if only they could find the spark that would set them into action. The missing links are the belief in oneself and the inspiration from others. Few of us believe that we are rich enough, smart enough, skilled enough, well enough connected, or "lucky" enough to achieve our dreams or effect change. So we settle for mediocrity, and this is uninspiring—not only for us, but also for everyone else with whom we connect.

Let's begin by thinking of ourselves as powerful, translating bold thoughts into bold actions, capable of making change anywhere we wish. The reality is that whatever we do changes the world—we simply need to decide the quality and scale of our purpose in life and therefore how much we will alter the course of the ship we call Earth. Jesus Christ, Mother Teresa, Mahatma Gandhi, Martin Luther King, Jr.—none of these were born with any special privilege. Indeed, they were likely born with less of everything than you and I. They did not complain—they simply committed to changing the world.

People who are effective (a term we will explore further in Reflection Eleven) inspire others, because it is inspiring to see people actually getting things done, rather than just talking about it. And the act of being effective is inspiring because we are a species that seeks completion and order. Loose ends and untidiness frustrate; conclusions and closures offer a sense of satisfaction and tidiness—an inner pleasure that flows from the completion of tasks, projects, or missions. The experience of effectiveness is intensely satisfying and inspiring.

To Be Inspiring, We Must Be Ambitious

What would it take to change the world? We would need to pull the levers that could make the most effective change in the shortest period of time. So, which levers would we pull? In a previous era, we might have reached for the *religious-community lever* because the religious community was the most revered and respected of all human communities. This is no longer so. As the power, influence, and credibility of the religious community waned, the political community assumed its role. But this eventually faded, too, and today, the most powerful community in our society has become business—it is now the business community that can influence the world more than any other. Indeed, if we wanted to change the world, the most effective way to do so would be to change the global impact of, for example, Wal-Mart (nearly 2 million employees), Manpower (employing nearly 4.5 million temporary and permanent staff), Deutsche Post, Siemens, Hon Hai Precision Industry (Hong Kong), and McDonald's (each with around 500,000 employees), all of whom have millions of suppliers and customers. Each week, 100 million people shop at Wal-Mart alone. Within the orbit of just these six typical large organizations, hundreds of millions—perhaps billions—of lives are touched daily. If the leaders of these six organizations were to convene and commit to changing the world by honoring and inspiring their employees more, being more mindful of how they impact their communities and the environment, how they deal with ethics and leadership, how they pay their taxes, how they regard the spirit, how they enrich the human experience, how they nourish meaning and fulfillment—in short, how they lead, inspire, and enhance lives—they would change the world. And they could change the world faster than any other single grouping of people or organizations.

Yet many corporate leaders misread this opportunity, resorting instead to tactics that may enhance short-term results at the expense of the common good. This is uninspiring to employees, customers, suppliers, regulators, unions—just about everybody— the very opposite of what we are intending to achieve. The results are continuing messes and disappointment with work and corporate life. The meltdowns of Wall Street and Detroit and the disarray of many industries are some recent examples. The disenchantment and irritation people feel is illustrated by the example of the wireless phone industry: about 85 percent of the U.S. population—more than 250 million Americans—use cell phones. According to a study by the Pew Internet & American Life Project, Americans would find it harder to abandon their cell phones than the Internet, television, or traditional landline phones. Meanwhile, the love affair Americans have with their cell phones is eclipsed by their loathing for the wireless companies. In 2008, the Better Business Bureau reported that out of the 3,900 industries it tracks, the wireless sector had received more complaints than any other for three straight years. Several states have filed lawsuits against wireless providers for unlawfully extending contracts without obtaining customers' consent, signing them up for expensive and unauthorized services and subscription fees, and failing to disclose fees, taxes, and other charges. Many states have resorted to introducing legislation that will mandate better behavior from cell companies. Of course, not all wireless companies, or their leaders, are ruthless. Many in the wireless industry see their work as noble, changing the world and connecting people in countless beneficial ways, and those who work for such inspiring leaders will not feel the alienation experienced by the rest of the industry—they will be inspired, and only inspired employees and customers become loyal champions and promoters of organizations.

A Corporation or a Movement?

Do this exercise with me for a moment: Take two pieces of paper and head one with the word "Corporation," and the other with the word "Movement." Now write down all the words that immediately come to your mind when you think of the idea of "a corporation." When you have completed this, do the same on the other page: what words come to your mind when you think of the idea of "a movement"? Chances are that on the "Corporation" page you wrote words like profit, bureaucracy, hierarchy, controls, politics, lawsuits, budgets, meetings, fear, policies, marketing ploys, regulators, and so on. On the page headed "Movement" you might have listed words like, passion, change, transformation, excitement, values, integrity, a cause, dreams, inspiration, progress, leadership, service, improvement, and so on.

Now ask yourself these questions: Which one am I trying to build? Which one inspires me?

Every team, every organization can be *a movement*. We can create institutions that stand for something, that will begin a revolution or a transformation, and that serve the world and make it a better place for us all. It is a choice. What will it be for you?

The Essential Self and the Social Self: Joy and Satisfaction

Osho said, "Your whole idea about yourself is borrowed—borrowed from those who have no idea of who they are themselves."

We are each comprised of what John Northam has called *the essential self* and *the social self*—or what in this book we will refer to as the Soul and the Personality. The personality is akin to the social self, and it is the exterior by which we are known to others. The essential self is a deeper, mystical source that connects us to the sacred. The metric we use when working from our social self is *success*—a measure that is *externally* gauged. The metric we use when working from our essential self is satisfaction—or what we might call *joy*—a measure that is *internally* gauged. The soul represents our true essence, our internal compass, what we long for and what, if supported generously by the personality, would guide us joyfully, and flawlessly, to what I will refer to later as our Destiny, Character, and Calling. But the personality constantly manipulates and overrides our thinking in order to make us conform to an external compass—what people will think, our image, our shortcomings, how we will be assessed or judged, what is politically correct, whether we will succeed or fail or be happy, or whether our actions will enhance our careers—in other words, our level of "success." Jonathan Winters once commented, "I couldn't wait for success, so I went ahead without it." So, although our lives succumb to the direction of the compass of our social self—an outside measure—we yearn to be guided more authentically from within, by our North Star, our essential self—an inside measure.

The soul falls in love—the personality calls it infatuation—and warns that the object of our desires is flawed, dangerous, unreliable, and sometimes unattractive. The soul wants to make the world a better place, but the personality whispers a thousand seductions in our ear—reasons why our idealism is naïve and doomed to failure. The soul wants us to be on Higher Ground—the personality heaps scorn upon us for being idealists.

The most frequently seen leadership style is one that emanates principally from the personality—what some might view as the ego, which is typically characterized by ambition, determination, aggression, and goal attainment, and this results in the dismal examples of self-interested leadership we referred to earlier. Living a life that is inspiring, and that inspires others, requires that we listen to the soul at least as often, perhaps even more, than we listen to our personality—hearing and respecting both equally. In other words, inspiring leadership, and being inspired, flows from joy—not success—from the soul more than the personality. (In Reflection Four, we will discuss the difference between joy and success and the different energies we experience that determine where we fall on the "joy-success" continuum.)

Defining Inspirational Leadership®[4]

How might the world look if we became *fully conscious*, inviting the Soul—the leader that resides within—to complement our learned leadership style? The result would be the practice of *inspirational leadership*, which we are all capable of, but which requires our conscious and ongoing commitment in order to achieve its full expression. Let's begin with a definition of this soul-based style of leadership, which will guide us throughout this book. Inspirational leadership must contain three essential components:

1. Loving intent
2. Contribution to the positive growth of others
3. Enhancing the condition of the world

This is how we could illustrate the framework:

---

[4] For a detailed overview of Inspirational Leadership, please see my book *Inspirational Leadership: Destiny, Calling and Cause*, The Secretan Center Inc., 2003

Therefore, Inspirational Leadership could be defined as follows:

> *Inspirational leadership is a serving relationship with others that inspires their growth and makes the world a better place.*

Inspirational leadership is falling in love with the process of inspiring others and leading them with passion and joy, continuously willing, and actively supporting, the good of the other. Leadership is not a formula or a model. It is not a "system" or a "process" that can be copied without connection to the heart. It is a way of *being*. And when it is inspiring, it flows from our essential self.

When we use the term "leader," it is meant to be synonymous with parent, teacher, executive, minister, politician, counselor, friend, son or daughter, husband or wife—even simply with "human being." We are *all* leaders. This is why the term "leadership" is so often used in such a sloppy way. We are all called to lead in almost every aspect and stage of our lives, and inspiring leadership is an essential ingredient of every part of life. Inspirational leadership builds relationships, forms friendships, changes thinking and philosophies, gives birth to new ideas, and shapes lives and hearts. As children, we are leaders—at school, in sports, in our pastimes, and in our friendships. As we grow and become parents, we are invited to assume new leadership responsibilities. We are called to lead at home, in our places of worship, in our corporations, in our communities, and in our countries. Inspirational leadership changes the world.

Leadership is an inside job. When we forget this, we are uninspiring. But when we remain conscious of the importance of leading from the inside, we are greatly inspired. Inspirational leadership flows from the soul and elevates the souls of others.

It is strange that we should attempt to lead with only the acquired superficiality of leadership skills that are principally found in our social self, our personality. And it is equally strange—and even unnerving—that we are prepared to live with the sadness that results when we allow the precious gifts of our essential self to die inside us while we are living, for a life that reflects only the personality is a life that fails to inspire. How might we touch the world if we became *fully conscious leaders,* totally awake and aware of our Destiny, Character, and Calling— our North Star, our sacred purpose for being in *this* point in space and time, with a full awareness that we are all one?

How did we forget who we are? And, having forgotten, how and why have we let *others* define for us who we are? Why have we handed over our power to others—authority figures, thought leaders, social norms, media stereotypes, or what our parents and teachers told us we needed to be? Surely, we are the best suited to make our own discoveries—with the counsel of others, of course— and our North Star must be the final arbiter. Our essence is the benchmark of our authenticity and integrity. And where will we find the answers? As we all know but seldom acknowledge, the answers lie within. As Sri Ramana Maharshi put it, "Happiness is your nature. It is not wrong to desire it. What is wrong is seeking it outside when it is inside." Of course, this does not mean to imply that the singular pursuit of happiness is the end game, either—as Viktor Frankl, psychiatrist and Auschwitz survivor, wrote in the classic *Man's Search for Meaning,* "…a human being is not one in pursuit of happiness but rather in search of a reason to become happy…" This, as we shall see, is a very important distinction.

Few of us have thought about why we have been placed on Earth—our *reason* to become happy—and, if we were asked this question, we might become strangely tongue-tied. But how can we inspire and lead others if we cannot even explain the reason for our own existence in the first place—the reason why we are here? Leadership is not the practice of manipulating, motivating, and controlling the behavior of others in order to achieve what we want. That is a leadership style that emanates from the personality—"old-story" leadership. Inspiring leadership is Higher Ground Leadership, and it is the practice of being an inspiration to others, drawing from our inner, authentic selves—and this emanates from the soul. Leadership is not so much something we learn; it is more something we *live*. We cannot "do" leadership. We *become* Higher Ground Leaders—it is something we express through *being*.

If we have no idea about what we are supposed to be doing while we are on this planet, then we cannot know the practical purpose and sacred intent of our lives. Therefore, whatever the form of leadership we practice, it will have no spiritual brilliance—the flame—to shine on the path that advances or justifies our life's purpose. As the Buddha said, "Just as a candle cannot burn without fire, men cannot live without a spiritual life."

Søren Kierkegaard, the great Danish philosopher, asked, "One sticks one's finger into the soil to tell by the smell in what land one is: I stick my finger in existence—it smells of nothing. Where am I? Who am I? How came I here? What is this thing called the world? What does this world mean? Who is it that has lured me into the world? Why was I not consulted, why not made acquainted with its manners and customs instead of throwing me into the ranks, as if I had been bought by a kidnapper, a dealer in souls? How did I obtain an interest in this big enterprise they call reality? Why should I have an interest in it? Is it not a voluntary concern? And if I am to be compelled to take part in it, where is the director? I should like to make a remark to him. Is there no director? Whither shall I turn with my complaint?"

At an instinctive level, we are all full of questions about our existence, but choose to put them in a little black box while we busy ourselves with the mundane, or reference our lives against external criteria—thus living from our social selves and ignoring our essential selves.

As W. H. Auden sardonically put it, "We are here on earth to do good for others. What the others are here for, I don't know." Of course, he had his tongue in his cheek, for he surely knew that others were here for the same purpose as he.

How can we tell that our leadership efforts are relevant to the purpose of our lives—to do good for others—to serve others? Surely the things we do on a day-to-day basis should lead to something meaningful, should serve others more than ourselves, and should come from the most authentic part of our being. When we lead, the effect of our leadership should amount to something, lead to something, change something, and make something better.

Without a sense of connection to a divine purpose or higher power, we will default into "leadership autopilot," practicing a way of leading that we may have learned by reading a CEO's biography or by watching film and TV heroes. Or we may measure our leadership effectiveness by referencing metrics that satisfy the social self but leave the essential self hungry. We need a deeper sense of who we are, and an acceptable balance between our social self and our essential self, following our North Star, to be fully present as conscious beings, before we can presume to lead others.

So often, leadership is practiced with much affectation—we learn "techniques" and "the tricks of the trade"— how to dress, what to say, how to make a speech, how to command attention, how to behave in a meeting, how to climb the corporate ladder, and an endless array of other superficialities. Through all this, the soul waits patiently while the personality asserts and indulges itself in its shallow journey. This is why leadership often gets such a bad press—it is practiced as a self-serving, social-self function instead of being the result of a powerful, integrity-centered passion. The truth is, nothing happens on Earth without the presence of leadership. But because the soul sits patiently in the shadow of the personality, it often remains unheard—suspended. Meanwhile, the personality engages in "doing" instead of "being." For many inspiring leaders, the personality is being awakened by a growing awareness of the soul, and is slowly beginning to respect and listen to it.

This is the difference between "old-story leadership" and "New-Story Leadership" that heralds the new era of inspiring leadership we are entering—the difference between working from the personality alone on the one hand, and aligning the personality and the soul on the other—the difference between doing and being, the difference between being unconscious and becoming conscious, the difference between carrot-and-stick methods and inspiring people. It is the difference between talking about leadership and being a Higher Ground Leader. In order to engage the soul, we must ask questions that go beyond the personality or the ego, such as, "What am I communicating when I am not speaking?" "What am I teaching when I am simply being"? "How can I serve?" "How can I make the world a better place?" And we must be rigorously objective with the answers we hear after asking these questions, and then determine if we are satisfied with them. Paul Tillich said, "Being religious means asking passionately the question of the meaning of our existence and being willing to receive answers, even if the answers hurt." Asking subtle, soul-centered questions like these is a sign that the leader within has been awakened, is becoming conscious, and is getting ready to lead others from a place of inner wisdom, authenticity, and integrity, rather than from a superficial, parroted approach to leadership that lacks substance and roots. As Rabbi Zusya so eloquently put it, "In the world to come, I shall not be asked, "Why were you not Moses?" I shall be asked, "Why were you not Zusya?""

And Sri Ramana Maharshi explains, "Nearly all mankind is more or less unhappy because nearly all do not know the true Self. Real happiness abides in Self-knowledge alone. All else is fleeting. To know one's Self is to be blissful always."

This is the journey we will now begin—the discovery of self, the journey that will inspire you, and therefore inspire others—the journey that adds inner metrics to the outer ones.

Reflection One: DESTINY

*When you are inspired by some great purpose,
some extraordinary project, all your thoughts break
their bonds; your mind transcends limitations, your
consciousness expands in every direction, and you
find yourself in a new, great and wonderful world.
Dormant forces, faculties and talents become alive,
and you discover yourself to be a greater person by
far than you ever dreamed yourself to be.*

Patanjali

Your North Star

Because the star Polaris, generally called the North Star, shines
directly onto Earth's North Pole, it has been used for centuries by
navigators as a guide when plotting a route in the northern hemi-
sphere. The same star is used as a navigational aid by many
species of birds, as well as by salmon, dolphins, and whales. The
North Star represents a fixed bearing in the sky which enables the
traveler to plot a route and stay on course.

During the early period of American history, when slavery
was prevalent, slaves seeking freedom from captivity knew it was
unsafe to escape in daylight, so they traveled by night. Having no
signposts or visible landmarks, they followed the North Star,
because they knew it would guide them to freedom. The slaves
passed a song among themselves that contained the coded direc-

tions for traveling north. It was called "Follow the Drinking Gourd." The "Drinking Gourd" refers to a hollowed-out gourd, which was frequently used by slaves and other rural Americans as a water dipper. It represented a code for the star formation of the Big Dipper, which points directly to the North Star or Polaris.

These freedom seekers knew that as long as they kept the North Star firmly in their sights, and remained centered on it, they would never be lost.

What is your North Star? What is the internal power that provides this strength of focus, clarity, and freedom in your life? What inspires you; what is the spark that lights your fire and keeps you directed? When you discover it, it will be the spark that begins the process of helping you to feel alive. This spark is ignited when you become aware of the deep passion residing in your Destiny, Character, and Calling. The spark is your inner knowing which, when it is revealed, is so certain, secure, and keen that it steers you towards your life's purpose. The spark is the radiance within you that makes you an inspiring being.

Passion Is the Authentic Guide for Our Choices

Eighteen-year-old Dustin Carter has no legs and almost no arms. In 2008, he qualified in Ohio's Division II wrestling tournament, finishing third in his region and staking a claim to being one of the best wrestlers in the state.

In the early days of wrestling, there were no rules—kicking, biting, gouging, and clawing were all part of the contest. Rules eventually emerged and today one of them is that, at the beginning of the contest, one wrestler's foot must be on one line on the mat, and one of the opponent's feet must be on the other.

Paul Branco recalls the first time he refereed one of Dustin's matches.

"I looked down to see just one foot on the green line and nothing on the red," he says. "So I asked the other wrestler to put his foot on the line. It turned out to be the Hillsboro [Ohio] wrestler with no legs, and he looks at me and says, 'Do you want me to go get a shoe?'"

Branco said he was "taken aback for an instant," and then told Dustin, "Just anywhere close to the line would be fine."

Said Branco, "Away we went...and Dustin won the match."

"His perseverance speaks for itself," said Scott Goodpaster, Carter's trainer. "He wants to win. He wakes up every day wanting to win. This is his passion, and he bleeds for it. He works so hard to get by in life."

When Dustin was five years old, he was stricken by a rare blood disease known as meningococcemia, which originates from the same bacterium that causes a severe form of meningitis. Typically, it kills 15 to 20 percent of patients. Some survivors suffer such extreme tissue damage that they require surgical treatment ranging from skin grafts to partial or full amputations of an arm or leg.

Dustin lost both arms and legs to amputation.

After his surgery at Cincinnati Shriners Hospital for Children, he underwent three months of rehabilitation. A week after leaving the hospital, he was attending a birthday party at his grandparents' house and while sitting on his dad's knee, he lost his balance. As he tried to catch himself with his hand, he suddenly realized—there was no hand there. His dad caught him before he hit the floor.

Dustin felt humiliated.

"Dad, I just wish it could be like it was," he said.

His dad, Russ Carter, says, with a tear in his eye, "It's the only time I've heard him complain. The only time."

Dustin Carter says, "I wrestle like anybody else. I go to school like anybody else. I can live on my own like anybody else. I can do anything anybody else can do. I don't like people feeling sorry for me." And they shouldn't—he unscrews water-bottle tops, pops aluminum tabs on soda cans, unwraps ham sandwiches,

writes essays, makes Western omelets, puts his pants on prosthetic legs every morning (a 15-minute task), mows the lawn,
swims, fishes, and, when he wrestles, he darts around the gym-
nasium floor like a Jack Russell on steroids. Dustin Carter's spark
just won't quit.

Douglas H. Everett once remarked, "There are some people
who live in a dream world, and there are some who face reality;
and then there are those who turn one into the other."

When she was 16, South African swimming sensation Natalie
Du Toit nearly qualified for the 2000 Sydney Olympics in three
events. The sports world sensed there were great things in store for
the strong, gritty swimmer. The 2004 Athens Olympics beckoned.

But in 2001, her world suddenly changed. After completing
her morning workout, Du Toit hopped onto her motor scooter
and slipped into the Monday rush-hour traffic and headed for
school. Within minutes, a careless driver emerged from a parking lot, careening directly into her left leg. The carnage was ugly;
the extent of her injuries became immediately obvious. "I kept
saying, 'I've lost my leg, I've lost my leg,'" remembers Du Toit.
Her teammates rushed to help her. Traffic clogged up and chaos
ensued. A motorcycle policeman speeding to the scene of the accident crashed headfirst into a truck, sustaining injuries that
required him to be airlifted to a hospital.

Du Toit has an irrepressible spark, too. She comes from solid
stock—her Mother, Deidre, is a receptionist and her father,
David, is a foreman—and they are a main source of her determination and grit. (Even the family dogs hint at the same qualities—Binga, a Boxer, and Storm, a Rottweiler).

The doctors struggled to save her leg without success, eventually amputating it through the left knee and inserting a tita-
nium rod into her broken femur.

"I remember asking my mom, 'When are they going to ampu-
tate?'" Du Toit reflects. "My mom's answer was that they already
had."

Her mind numbed with medication, Du Toit vaguely absorbed the news. The following day she got out of bed—her North Star was calling.

"I just wanted to get back to life again—swimming four hours a day—and I wanted to be able to walk again so that I would be able to do things by myself," she says.

Her friends, family, and teammates visited her in the hospital and self-consciously offered their good wishes. She enjoyed receiving visitors, but recoiled at the pity. So she freaked out her visitors by raising the sheets and revealing her half leg. Some almost fainted. This was not a spiteful action, but an indication of the defiant spirit burning within—her North Star asserting itself.

Whenever Du Toit is racing at an event, one will find an inspired crowd standing and cheering. What they are witnessing in the pool is a champion who happens to be an amputee—and is leading the pack. The crowd is thrilled and vocal with their admiration for this athlete whose North Star shines so brightly that it inspires them and fills them with awe.

Natalie Du Toit is one of the world's fastest distance swimmers. Less than two years after the accident, she qualified for the finals of the 800-meter freestyle at the 2002 Commonwealth Games, marking the first time an amputee in the modern era had raced in the finals of an able-bodied international swimming competition.

Du Toit has as much—perhaps more—stamina than any other Olympian on the planet. "I can swim an 800 meters, I can swim 1500 meters, or a 5 km, or a 10 km, and I can go the same pace the whole way," Du Toit said. "No matter if I am hurting or in pain, I go 1 min 11 sec [for every 100 meters]." How does she do it? "It's just training and training," she says. "Obviously I know I don't have the sprint, so I have to put in as much effort as possible in the middle. On the 10 km, I cramp easily on my hamstring—you can feel a massive knot in my hamstring always. I could feel the cramp in that 10 km in Seville [Open Water World Swimming Championships, May 2008, where she placed fourth], so I had to rely on my arms." Natalie Du Toit participated in both the able-bodied Olympics and the Paralympic Games in Beijing, placing 16th in the 10-km open-water race and winning five gold medals in the Paralympic Games. She says, "...the tragedy of life does not lie in not reaching your goals. The tragedy of life lies in not having goals to reach for. It is not a disgrace not to reach the stars, but it is a disgrace not to have stars to reach for." For Natalie Du Toit, the most important star is her North Star.

Another South African, Oscar Pistorius, has been dubbed by London's *Daily Mail* "the fastest man on no legs." With the aid of high-tech carbon-fiber blades known as Cheetahs, he is as fast as the best able-bodied runners in the world and a Paralympic champion and world-record holder in amputee races over 100 m, 200 m, and 400 m, as well as being a gold-medal winner in Athens. In January 2008, the IAAF[5] ruled that Pistorius, known as the "blade runner," was ineligible to compete in the Beijing Olympics because, in their opinion, his prosthetic racing legs *gave him a clear competitive advantage*! But five months later, an ecstatic Pistorius won his appeal of the decision from the Court of Arbitration for Sport in Lausanne, Switzerland, and was granted eligibility to compete in the Olympics.

But despite coming third and running a personal best time of 46.25 seconds at the Spitzen Leichtathletik meeting in Lucerne on July 16, 2008, Pistorius failed in his final opportunity to qualify for the 400 meters at the 2008 Summer Olympics by 0.70 seconds. Athletics South Africa later announced that he would also not be selected for the 4 x 400 meters relay team as four other runners had better times. If Pistorius had been picked, he would have become the first leg amputee runner to participate in the Olympic Games. While he did not succeed in qualifying for the

---

[5] International Association of Athletics Federations

2008 Olympics, he brought home three gold medals from the Paralympic Games for the 100-, 200-, and 400-meter sprints.

When he was asked about the possibility of the IAAF offering him a wild card to take part in the Olympics, Pistorius responded, "I do not believe that I would accept. If I have to take part in the Beijing Games, I should do it because I qualified." Instead, he expressed a preference for focusing on being selected to represent South Africa in the 2012 Summer Olympics in London, noting that it was a more realistic target, as "Sprinters usually reach their peak between 26 and 29. I will be 25 in London and I'll also have two, three years' preparation."

"People ask me all the time if I wish I had the rest of my legs," says Pistorius. "No. I guess it's a kind of an inconvenience, having to put on different legs to do different things, but there's nothing that anyone else can do that I can't do." Oscar Pistorius' spark just won't quit, either.

Sri Chinmoy wrote, "The determination in your heroic effort will permeate your mind and heart even after your success or failure is long forgotten."

The common characteristic that Dustin Carter, Natalie Du Toit, and Oscar Pistorius share is the spark that becomes their North Star—they all have absolute clarity about who they are and what they want to do with their lives—so much clarity, in fact, that able-bodied athletes are *intimidated* by them, attempting to exclude them from competing by protesting that *they* have an unfair advantage! Reflect on this a minute: people who, to most of us, would seem to be disadvantaged, suddenly take on the capacity to win, to excel beyond us, because the bright spark of their focus—their North Star—is so powerful, it shines brighter sometimes than some of us can handle.

The Power of a North Star in the Corporate Setting

Mike McCallister is the President and Chief Executive Officer of Humana Inc., a Fortune 100 company and one of America's leading providers of health benefits. Shortly after President Barack Obama took office, health insurance became the most important social issue since civil rights in the 1960s, and activists of various persuasions demonized health insurers. The future of health care in America, and therefore of Humana, was thrown into question. With 30,000 employees, $30 billion in sales, and 12 million people insured, Humana is a heavyweight and touches the lives of families everywhere in America.

Mike McCallister joined Humana in 1974 and assumed the roles of president and CEO in 2000. In 2006, he was rated by Forbes Magazine as one of the most successful CEOs in American business at creating shareholder value.

When the environment is turbulent, maintaining equilibrium and focus is a critical part of a leader's responsibility. Mike was forced to deal calmly and simultaneously with many issues on many fronts, but through it all, he ensured that his leadership team, and all of Humana's employees, retained their optimism, focus, and commitment to customer service. Among other priorities, he saw his role as providing stability and direction and thus inspiring his colleagues while ensuring that external distractions did not unnerve people—inside or outside the organization. Author John Keegan might have been describing Mike McCallister as much as Ulysses S. Grant when he wrote: "Grant did not affect to be a high-level strategic thinker. Nothing in his manner or appearance suggested he was anything other than a common-sense, down-to-earth fighting soldier. Common sense and down-to-earthness are among the most valuable qualities, however, a strategist can possess, and he possessed them in abundance."[6]

As we worked together, we helped Humana to develop ONE Dream™—a methodology for defining intense clarity and a grand vision of the future, that if kept firmly in the center of everything, provides flawless navigation through turbulence (more on this in Reflection Five).

---

[6] Keegan, John, "The American Civil War: A Military History," Knopf, 2009

I will share the process for developing your own Destiny, Character, and Calling Statements later in this Reflection, but here is how Mike McCallister defined his own—his personal North Star—that guided his leadership behavior during turbulent times:

> *Destiny:* To provide leadership in health care that respects people and the environment
> *Character:* To be a builder of an environment of integrity, respect, and calm in all circumstances
> *Calling:* To provide visionary, transformational leadership in health care

Mike has become a hero to many for his unswerving and inspiring guidance during challenging and difficult times. The continued success of Humana is testament to his leadership, which is derived from having a clear inner sense of why he is here, how he will be, and what he will do—his *Why-Be-Do*—and from the power of this inner knowing comes his ability to inspire others.

In these examples, and many others, we are reminded that passion and clarity—when laser-like in their intensity—lead to effective and inspiring lives. Humana is successful, despite the surrounding challenges, because Mike McCallister is inspiring, and he is inspiring because he is guided by his North Star. When we have this clear inner knowing, all obstacles—even extreme physical limitations or adverse business conditions—become inconsequential. Sarah Reinertsen, for instance, shrugged off adversity, becoming the first female amputee to compete in and conquer the Ford Ironman Triathlon Kona (a 2.4-mile swim, 112-mile bike ride, and 26.2-mile run)—an astounding feat. "My dream is to do extraordinary things every day," she says. Kyle Maynard, who suffers from a congenital defect that robbed him of his arms from above the elbows and his legs from above the knees, follows the motto, "It's not what I can do, but what I will do." That is the attitude that has spurred him to become a winning high-school wrestler, weightlifter, and gifted student—and an inspiration to everyone who knows him.

Our North Star is our Destiny, Character, and Calling—the reason why we are here on this planet. It is the spark within us that guides our lives, makes us vibrant, and causes us to be inspiring leaders and role models for others. It is the spark that renders obstacles mere "inconveniences," as Oscar Pistorius calls them. It is the voice inside—the passion—that invites us to have no excuses. *It is the voice of our soul.*

Destiny: The Soul's Call

The passion within us—our North Star—is what others find inspiring. Because it inspires us, it inspires others. And we are inspired because *they* are inspired. And so a magical cycle is created. It begins with an awareness of our Destiny.

Like Mike McCallister, every great leader in history, whether they were famous or not, knew their Destiny—the uniqueness within them that yearned to be lived. A person who has this spark, this passionate knowing, radiates it to others. They can't help themselves. The passionate energy of an inspired leader inspires others because they *experience it* as it illuminates their conversation, their relationship, their enjoyment of being with this person.

And leaders inspire when they approach all activities with a grand aspiration, connecting the dots from the activity, task, or communication to a much larger picture. Uninspiring leaders see tasks solely in terms of a metric—Will it make money? Will it help us achieve the budget? Will we get the sale? Will we meet our quality standards? Is it legal? Will it make the analysts happy?

While all of these measures may have merit in the appropriate situations, their energy vibrates at a frequency below our passion threshold, and they are questions that seldom inspire. Inspiring leaders see everything in terms of how a task or action will change the world and make it a better place. An intention to honor the sacredness of others and the world is embedded in all of their communications—it is part of their relational DNA. While we can easily argue about metrics, such arguments shrivel in the presence of a noble cause, a dream, or a grand ambition to make a difference in the lives of others (see Reflection Five). Such aspirations, held deeply in a sacred place in our hearts, represent our personal Destiny.

How can we find this hidden treasure that lies so deeply buried within us yet holds the power to ignite our spark, free our deepest passion, and reveal our Destiny to us? Years of conditioning by external influences and life's endless demands make many people numb to the small but powerful voice within—the voice of the soul. How can we learn to hear it again and accept its invitation to give expression to its call? In our work over many years with individuals and groups from many parts of the globe and from all walks of life, we have developed a set of simple exercises that have proven to be extraordinarily effective in revealing a person's Destiny, Character, and Calling—like Mike McCallister's at Humana. These exercises can be completed alone or in a group setting, and they will benefit you most if you select a time in which you will not be rushed or distracted by the cares of your day. Allow the voice of your soul to speak and guide you to the discovery of a lifetime—the full awareness of why you are here and what you truly want to do with your life!

We will now approach the first of these exercises to help you create your Destiny Statement.

Creating a Destiny Statement

We have conducted hundreds of workshops in which participants have discovered their Destiny, and it is enormously gratifying to watch the self-discovery and liberation that are released when that spark is ignited by the newly revealed passion that has lain dormant within many of the participants. One woman said that apart from giving birth to her daughter, this was the most exciting experience of her entire life.

How do we define a Destiny Statement?

Here is a simple but dramatic process that we have designed to unfold this for you.

There are two givens that we all share:

1. Our passion is drawn to the things that excite us—positively and negatively; and
2. At our core, we all yearn to serve and improve the world.

So, what excites you? We have developed a paradoxical process that will help you to find out:

Very often it is the shadow just as much as the light that engages us. We are animated by what inspires us just as much as by what repulses or shocks us. In the spaces below, write down two things that you feel are *wrong* with the world—we will call these *Terrathreats*—the shadows of the world. These are issues that you consider to be so serious that unless they are resolved, they will be radically detrimental to the world and might even cause the demise of humanity and the Earth. Friedrich Nietzsche said, "He who has a why to live for can bear almost any how."

One more thing before you begin to write: You may be thinking, "Oh, I'm just little ole' me—I can't change the world." But reflect on Bernard Shaw's words, "This is the true joy in life: Being used for a purpose recognized by yourself as a mighty one, being a force of nature instead of a feverish, selfish little clod of ailments and grievances, complaining that the world will not devote itself to making you happy. I am of the opinion that my life belongs to the whole community and as long as I live, it is my privilege to do for it what I can. It is a sort of splendid torch which I have got hold of for the moment, and I want to make it

burn as brightly as possible before handing it on to future generations."

As I observed earlier, many people who changed the world
came from very humble beginnings—Jesus Christ, Mahatma
Gandhi, Martin Luther King, Jr., Nelson Mandela, Mother
Teresa—none of these were privileged or powerful, they simply
had a burning inner passion, "a splendid torch," as Bernard
Shaw put it. They had a spark—a North Star—to address the
wrongs of the world. So why not you? You are starting with even
greater advantages than they had.

In the spaces below, write down two things that spoil the
world for you—your Terrathreats—and that hold the potential to
threaten or wound the world, and to cause serious global damage if we don't change or reverse them:

My Terrathreats are: (Step 1)

1. _____

2. _____

Now, distill these two *Terrathreats* into one word if you can—
or at least no more than two:

My Terrathreats are: (Step 2)

_____

_____

Now write the *opposite* of these words in the spaces below—
not an interpretation or paraphrasing—but the *exact* opposite
word, the antonym. For example, the opposite of hatred would
be love, or of poverty would be abundance, and so on. We call
these "exact opposites" *Terrafixes*:

My Terrafix(es) is (are):

Now craft this Terrafix (or several if you wish, but try to keep their number small) into a statement that describes how you wish to dedicate your life (see Mike McCallister's example on p. 40.) Are you prepared to live your life in service of this Destiny Statement?

Here is how it is done: Shirley Willihnganz is the Executive Vice President and Provost of the University of Louisville. Shirley identified her Terrathreats as loneliness, alienation, and despair, and therefore her matching Terrafixes were joy, closeness, and hope. Elizabeth Gilbert said, "The inability to open up to hope is what blocks trust, and blocked trust is the reason for blighted dreams." From these Terrathreats, Shirley fashioned a Destiny Statement:

To create a more joyful world

For Shirley, the word "joy" embraced all of her Terrafixes, and so she settled on just that one word because she felt it both captured her passion and was efficient. We will continue to follow Shirley's progress with the development of her Why-Be-Do in the next two Reflections.

Here are a few more examples to inspire your creative juices and for you to use as a model—note the brevity:

To help create a sustainable and abundant world
Scott Spiker, CEO, First Command Financial Services

To nurture a world that empowers others to make their contribution
Marty Durbin, President, First Command Financial Services

To illuminate the beauty of every soul
Julie Snyder, Secretan Center Faculty Member

To help create a more loving and serving planet
Ken Jacobsen, Secretan Center Faculty Member

To create more learning, love and peace in the world
Deb Gmelin, Corporate Director, The Leadership Institute, Humana Inc.

To elevate self-esteem in society
Wally Amos (Inventor of Famous Amos Chocolate Chip Cookies)

To make the world simpler
Ed Boudreau, Secretan Center Faculty Member, ER Physician, and Six Sigma Black Belt

And my own, which is:

To help create a more sustainable and loving planet

Now write yours:

My Destiny Statement is:

_____

_____

Marvel at these words for a moment!
You have created an awesome thing—a definition of the rea-son why you are here and how you plan to live your life from here on in. This is the beginning of your spark. It is going to light your fire. Few people arrive at this clarity at any time in their lives. Savor the inspiration, the liberation, and the centering feel-ing it offers you. Celebrate it privately first, and, when you are ready, with your loved ones. Then celebrate it with everyone you

trust and those whom you wish to inspire. Share it with your colleagues and those whom you lead, teach, and coach—they will be inspired by your Destiny Statement. Explain to them that this is why you are here on Earth, this is why and how you lead, this is your essential self revealed, and this is who you are. Eventually, when you are ready, and as you hone and polish it, share it with the world.

Over the next few months, these words—so vital to the future of your life, and therefore the quality of your leadership—will fit increasingly snugly into your soul. Perhaps you may find a word a little awkward here and there, and you may need to "tweak" some of the language and make it a perfect fit for you—this is normal because this is a continuous process. But the core idea of your Destiny has now been revealed!

Resolve to be thyself: and know, that he who finds himself, loses his misery.

Matthew Arnold

Reflection Two: CHARACTER

All men and women are born, live, suffer and die;
what distinguishes us one from another is our dreams,
whether they be dreams about worldly or unworldly
things, and what we do to make them come about...
We do not choose to be born. We do not choose our
parents. We do not choose our historical epoch, the
country of our birth, or the immediate circumstances
of our upbringing. We do not, most of us, choose to
die; nor do we choose the time and conditions of
our death. But within this realm of choicelessness,
we do choose how we live.

Joseph Epstein

In the last Reflection, you accomplished something very few people ever do in their entire lives—you developed clarity about your life's Destiny—*why* you are here on this Earth. This is the first step in igniting the spark that will excite and inspire you, and this energy will transmit to others—you will radiate your inspiration. Many people have developed mission statements or can recite a homily about their life goals: to retire by 50, to provide for their children, to run a big company, to contribute to their community. These are all noble and worthy goals, but mission statements are an outdated methodology that served the old paradigm of fear-based, carrot-and-stick leadership built on competitive, dog-eat-dog precepts of corporate and personal behavior—the "old story of leadership." Understanding and following our Destiny, on the other hand, enables us to reach for more than mere targets of material success and ego-driven objectives—it connects us to the energy of the entire universe, expressed as the inner wisdom that directs our individual and collective lives.

Character and How We Serve

One of the great gifts that come with knowing one's Destiny is the awareness that we are here to serve. Paul said we should "serve one another in love" (Galatians 5:13). And Sri Sathya Sai Baba said, "Serve man until you see God in all men." It is by serving each other that we serve God. All major philosophies and religions support this concept, which is also an ideal to which effective societies and organizations aspire.[7] So, if our highest purpose while we are here on Earth is to serve each other (and therefore God, who is within each of us), how are we to do this, and how can we determine our own unique Character that will enable us to do so in a way that inspires?

We serve each other, and the larger collective—Earth, the universe, God—not through the *doing* that is described in so much of our goal-oriented management literature and teaching, but more through the *being: who* we are; not through our accomplishments, but through our presence; not from our *social* self, but through our *essential* self; not through our egos, but through our integrity; not just through the force of our personality, but through the radiance of our soul. Character is how we choose to *be*—particularly when we think no one is looking. As Dwight L. Moody once remarked, "Character is what you are in the dark."

So, our Character describes the way we want to be in the world, the ways in which we wish to touch others' lives and set an example. It describes how we want to be remembered—our moral legacy. Abraham Lincoln put it this way: "Character is like a tree and reputation like its shadow. The shadow is what we think of it; the tree is the real thing." How will your tree grow, and what shadow will it cast?

---

[7] The concept of Service is discussed in greater detail in Reflection Eight.

When considering the attributes of people who are inspiring, those that define the ego or the personality are numerous and quickly come to mind—ambition, vision, focus, determination, strength, power, dominance, skills—to name a few. But we seldom identify the inspiring leadership attributes that reside in the soul in the same way. In fact, to the untrained or unconscious ear, these are sometimes described as "weak," "soft," or "fluff," but to the inspired and inspiring leader, they are the opposite.

Merriam-Webster defines Character as "one of the attributes or features that make up and distinguish an individual; the complex of mental and ethical traits marking and often individualizing a person, group, or nation; main or essential nature." Theodore Roosevelt described it this way: "Character, in the long run, is the decisive factor in the life of an individual and of nations alike." Our Character Statement describes how we want to *be* in the world—how we want to *live* in order to make a difference, how we can be most effective in relating with others and nature, how we make the world better, how we become more inspiring, to ourselves and to others, as much of the time as possible—or even a bit more! Note the emphasis on *living* our Character—as High Eagle wrote, "The mere possession of a vision is not the same as living it, nor can we encourage others with it if we do not, ourselves, understand and follow its truths. The pattern of the Great Spirit is over us all, but if we follow our own spirits from within, our pattern becomes clearer. For centuries, others have sought their visions. They prepare themselves, so that if the Creator desires them to know their life's purpose, then a vision would be revealed. To be blessed with visions is not enough...we must live them!"

When our time comes, we leave behind our fame and material possessions, but we take our Character with us.

Defining a Character Statement

Our task, then, is to craft a clear definition—our Character Statement—that describes how we will *be* as we serve and fulfill our

Destiny. Let me walk you through the process of creating such a Character Statement by using the example of my own.

I have a tendency to be judgmental. I have opinions about everything from how toothpaste should be squeezed out of the tube to how the judges should vote on *American Idol* and how the President of the United States should run the country and interact with the world. Note the overuse of the word "should." In my private moments, I even have opinions about how God should improve! These judgments—which, of course, come straight from my ego—can easily slip into "right" and "wrong" statements, making some people "good" and others "bad." Of course, this is not always the most endearing or productive practice, and it sometimes damages relationships because it creates separateness, not oneness—judgment is a weapon that divides. At its worst, it alienates people, and at its best, it helps me to learn that others experience it as uninspiring and unloving.

What I am discovering from all this is that being a judgmental or critical person does not come across to others as a loving way to be, regardless of my intentions. In my role as a leader, I have found that if I want to guide the behavior of others, and if I wish to galvanize a team into action or to follow a strategy, I must first love them—and be sure my actions show that I love them—and from this loving place, I am then more able to inspire them. As a spouse, if I wish to build a solid, lifelong relationship with my partner, I must love her and inspire her every day. As a father, if I want the best for my children, I must love them and be an inspiring influence on them. As a friend, I must love the other and be so inspiring that they seek my company. If I want to change the world, I need to love others so much that they are inspired to change the world, to work for the greater good, and to achieve something of significance.

Reflecting on what I do that gets in my own way and diminishes the level of fulfillment and meaning I achieve in my life leads to a greater awareness of how I *need* to be. Or, put more positively, it informs me about how I will choose to live my life—

how I *will* be—so that it contributes to creating the kind of world I long for. I realize that I will not attain a perfect state in this aspiration, but, most days, I try my best. My personal discovery, then, is that I can be most effective in the world if, and when, I am a loving and inspiring person. So, this reveals the Character traits I want to embody—the definition of how I wish to *be*—and so I choose:

To be an inspiring and loving person

This, then, becomes my Character Statement. How can I seriously expect to influence others or have a positive effect on them—contrary to much of what we teach and the media portrays—from any place that is negative, coercive, sarcastic, manipulative, diminishing, selfish, political, pressuring, authoritarian, pushy, aggressive, ambitious, dishonest, nagging, browbeating, blustering, or dominating? These are all "push" behaviors, so frequently used in our society and in our leadership theories.

But the more I *push*, the more I invoke Newton's Third Law of Mechanics: *Every action has an equal and opposite reaction.* Therefore, the more I push, the more I will be *pushed back.* On the other hand, the more I am open—that is, *loving*—the more I will inspire others to the common good, and, using the same Law of Mechanics, the more I will invite reciprocal energy. So, if my Character invokes advantages for the common good—if I am loving and inspiring—I will attract others to join me on the same path. We call this leadership. It is the art of getting things accomplished through others—by loving and inspiring them—in order to make a positive influence on the world.

A Passion for Living with Strong Character

Scottish percussionist and composer Evelyn Glennie lost nearly all of her hearing by age 12. Instead of becoming isolated from what and whom she loved—separateness—she has used her hearing loss as a way to develop her Character and a unique connection to her music—oneness.

Evelyn Glennie was born in Aberdeenshire, Scotland, and raised on a farm there. Her father was Herbert Arthur Glennie, an accordionist in a Scottish country-dance band, and the strong, indigenous musical traditions of northeast Scotland played an important role in young Evelyn's development. Other major influences were Glenn Gould, Jacqueline du Pré, and Trilok Gurtu. The first instruments she played were the mouth organ and the clarinet.

Her entry into the world of music was anything but smooth. After studying at the Ellon Academy, she applied for admission to the Royal Academy of Music, but was turned down on the grounds that she could not possibly be a musician if she couldn't hear the music. They should have known better. The fiery Evelyn protested, asserting that she believed that young musicians should be selected for admission based solely on their ability to play music and not on whether they were missing some or all of their arms, legs, sight, or hearing. No lack of spark here. Somewhat taken aback by this feistiness, the Royal Academy ultimately accepted Evelyn Glennie, whose bold action forever changed the criteria by which not only young musicians, but all applicants, are selected for admission to schools, colleges, and training programs.

Evelyn Glennie excelled, becoming the first deaf person in musical history to successfully create and sustain a full-time career as a solo percussionist.

She gives more than a hundred performances annually worldwide, spending over four months in the United States, and performs with the greatest conductors, orchestras, and artists in the world. For the first ten years of her career, she was a pioneer in almost everything she did. In a live performance these days, she can use up to 60 instruments. She also plays the Great Highland Bagpipes and has her own registered tartan known as "The

Rhythms of Evelyn Glennie." She has collaborated with, among others, Nana Vasconcelos, Kodo, Bela Fleck, Bjork, Bobby McFerrin, Sting, Emanuel Ax, the King's Singers, the Mormon Tabernacle Choir, and Fred Frith. She has commissioned over 160 new works for solo percussion from many of the world's most eminent composers and has herself composed 53 concertos, 56 recital pieces, 18 concert pieces, and two works for percussion ensemble. She writes scores for film and television, having won two Grammys, and her first high-quality drama produced a score so original she was nominated for a British Academy of Film and Television Arts (BAFTA) award, which in the United Kingdom is equivalent to the American Oscars.

Glennie is considered to be profoundly deaf—meaning that she has some very limited hearing. She says that of the 100 or so articles that are written about her each year, the majority of them devote more ink to her hearing impairment than her performances. She believes that the media and the public misunderstand deafness, thinking that it simply means that a person cannot hear. Glennie's deafness, however, has not inhibited her ability to perform at the international level—her spark is too bright—she has simply taught herself to hear with parts of her body other than her ears. She regularly plays barefoot for both live performances and studio recordings, to better "feel" the music.

She explains, "Hearing is basically a specialized form of touch. Sound is simply vibrating air which the ear picks up and converts to electrical signals, which are then interpreted by the brain. The sense of hearing is not the only sense that can do this, touch can do this, too. If you are standing by the road and a large truck goes by, do you hear or feel the vibration? The answer is both. With very low frequency vibration, the ear starts becoming inefficient and the rest of the body's sense of touch starts to take over. For some reason, we tend to make a distinction between hearing a sound and feeling a vibration; in reality they are the same thing. It is interesting to note that in the Italian language this distinction does not exist. The verb 'sentire' means to hear and the same verb in the reflexive form, 'sentirsi,' means to feel. Deafness does not mean that you can't hear, only that there is something wrong with the ears. Even someone who is totally deaf can still hear/feel sounds."

Evelyn Glennie's life energy is invested in being able to "teach the world to listen." One can understand the motivation and the passion behind her mantra of *"making the difference"*—nothing means more to her—and this is how she wants to "be" in her life. She has chosen to model the behavior she is seeking in others by overcoming a perceived impairment and showing that, in reality, it is not an impairment. She is aware that she can influence the world most powerfully by being, as Gandhi put it, the change she wishes to see in the world. It comes from within her and emanates to others and inspires them. It is a spark that others recognize and find personally empowering. Her life is dedicated to bringing this message of awareness to people, inviting them to be more inclusive of those who are hearing-impaired, and demonstrating for all of us to how to learn to listen better and with more awareness.

From Evelyn Glennie's example, we can see that Character is a way of being that comes from our center, from a place deep inside, our essential self, and it represents our essence—how we want to be more than anything else—because we believe in it passionately and because we want the world to be better through the expression of our Character, our presence and being.

Creating Your Own Character Statement

What is your Character? How do you wish to "be" in this life? How will you live in order to inspire yourself and therefore others?

Here are a few examples to inspire your creative juices and for you to use as a model—again, note the brevity:

To be present to love and support my family with an everyday expanding consciousness
Francisco Moisés, Industry Director, Microsoft

To acknowledge and honor the sacred magnificence in all creation
Shonnie Lavender, Leadership Coach

To inspire people and organizations to positively grow through releasing and sharing their energy-flow
Mike Sturm, Developer of the 5 Dynamics Tool

To touch hearts and inspire souls with beauty and wisdom
Rob Ryder, Vice President of Learning and Leadership Development, Centura Health

To serve as an example and teacher of non-violent patterns in all areas of life
Skip Turner, Health Care Executive

To live with love, joy and passion
Robin Mooney, Sales Executive, Herman Miller

To be a creative, courageous and authentic leader
Tracey Gilmore, The Secretan Center

To be authentic, compassionate and serving
Ken Jacobsen, Secretan Center Faculty Member

To be an inspiring, joyful, loving person
Deb Gmelin, Corporate Director, The Leadership Institute, Humana Inc.

To be an open-hearted and caring role model
Ron Mandel, Secretan Center Faculty Member

...and my own...
To be an inspiring and loving person

Rob Ryder, whose Character Statement is shown above, says, "I refer to this statement constantly both in public and for myself. It defines my life, not just my work, and I find comfort in having it as a compass as I plot my course through whatever life happens to be throwing at me in any given moment. In many ways, it is an affirmation of what I am and what I aspire to. I have not changed it at all since getting comfortable with it in 2003."

Francisco Moisés, whose Character Statement also appears above, describes the focusing power of his Destiny, Character, and Calling Statements this way: "We all live and contribute in an amazing time of corporate and personal leadership evolution. By working on my Destiny, Character, and Calling, I increased my awareness of what is really important for me and the overall effectiveness in multiple aspects of my life."

Our Character Statement, as well as our Destiny and Calling Statements, may evolve over time and require refinement or revisions. For example, Sister Nancy Hoffman, former vice president of Mission, Centura Health, originally formulated her Character statement as follows:

To strive to act justly and love tenderly in all situations

Sometime later, she revised it to:

To act justly and love tenderly in all situations

Notice the elimination of the words "to strive." Sister Nancy Hoffman explains, "I have become very intentional and focused in my life, using my Destiny, Character, and Calling (Why-Be-Do) as a guide to how I wish to *be* in this world of form. I wish to *be* God's unconditional love for all of creation, I wish to *be* peace, I wish to *be* just, and I wish to *be* love. No more trying or striving, just present-moment *being*. Sound too radical and/or Eastern for a Catholic nun? So be it!"

Now write your own Character Statement—how do you want to "be" in this world? How do you wish to live your life? What qualities do you want to live by so that they are an inspiring beacon and model for others? How will you "be" so that others will look to you as their role model, the epitome of what they wish to become? How do you want to be remembered at the end of your life—how do you hope others will describe your character?

One more thing: try to be brief—eight to ten words or less. You may think that it can't be done, but remember that Ernest Hemingway once wrote a story in just six words—"For sale: baby shoes, never worn."—and is said to have called it his best work.

If we look to Shirley Willihnganz as our guide again, you will remember that her Destiny Statement is, **To create a more joyful world.** As you will recall, "hope" and "joy" resonate strongly for Shirley—both in her Terrafixes and in her Destiny Statement. Therefore, she has chosen to model the behavior she wishes to see in the world, in the belief that bringing about the Terrafix, and inspiring others towards it, will be easier if she is a living example. So, this is the kind of person she wishes to be, this is how she wants others to know her—this is her Character Statement:

To be a hopeful and joyful person

Now write yours:

My Character Statement is:

_____

_____

You can tell a lot about a fellow's character by his way of eating jelly beans.

Ronald Reagan

Reflection Three: CALLING

Your profession is not what brings home your paycheck. Your profession is what you were put on earth to do. With such passion and such intensity that it becomes spiritual in calling.

Vincent Van Gogh

Many people work in order to make a living—only an inspired minority are living fully because they *love* their work.

A Calling is the pursuit of a vocation that inspires; it is living a dream; it is the experience of radiant relevance.

Recently, I was working with a local community that had asked me to help them become a world-class center for entrepreneurs and technology experts. They wanted to be a magnet for cutting-edge thinkers and creative entrepreneurs who lived elsewhere but would relocate to their community, thus helping them to become a center of innovation and excellence. During our sessions, I invited them to develop a clear definition of why they exist, how they will be, and how they will use their gifts to serve—their Destiny, Character, and Calling Statements. This enabled each of them to describe their uniqueness and helped them to contribute to the building of an international reputation that would attract the talent they sought. In the course of my work with them, each of the 400 leaders participating in the conference was able to develop their own personal Destiny, Character, and Calling Statements to ensure that there was a tight alignment between their own personal dreams and those of their community. This is how teams are guided to greatness. (The importance of one shared dream in organizations is discussed in Reflection Five.)

One of the participants, Leo Deveau, was struggling. He was a market researcher, but he had not yet found his true Calling. I asked him where his passion lay, and after some hesitation, in which he seemed to fumble for an appropriate "business" response, he described his love of music. During our lunch break, some of the participants took me aside to explain that this man was a brilliant musician. So, I asked Leo if he would like to play for the audience at the end of our meal and, reluctantly, he agreed. Since we were in a theater, I reasoned that we might find a piano somewhere, and we did, and with the help of two stage hands, we lugged it into the lunch area.

After lunch, Leo sat down at the piano—and he let it rip! For a moment it seemed that Jerry Lee Lewis had just set fire to the piano. Leo raised the roof! Everyone could sense that he had come alive—this was a moment of pure joy for him as he rocked the room—this market researcher had morphed into a rock star. The audience erupted into a dancing, clapping, and whistling frenzy—a sea of inspired grins.

Leo ended his virtuoso performance with a flourish, and I thanked him. As the lengthy applause subsided, we all returned to the auditorium to continue our meeting. Before we began, I asked the audience, "Can anyone help Leo define his true Calling?" and they erupted into cheers, chanting, "Music! Music! Music!" Then I turned to Leo and said, "Are you still unclear about your Calling?"

Sometime later, Leo told me, "This experience enabled me to recognize and honor the God-given talent I have, and to pay attention to it and how I used it in my life. This didn't mean that I had to go out and form a band or create a CD, but rather, it showed me the importance of respecting it, identifying why it was a missing part of my life up to that point, and to begin to integrate it more fully into various aspects of my life.

"After that experience, I bought a full digital keyboard, and I have had a number of occasions to play publicly as well. Also, I've picked up playing the bodhran (an Irish frame drum), which I have been playing in a pub session band for the past couple of years. It's a lot easier to carry around, compared to a piano! As I think back on the experience I had with you, I've come to recognize and value in a deeper way the role of music and playing an instrument in my life. It is a key part of who I am!"

We can all take our passion and turn it into our Calling. Indeed, living a life in which we avoid or deny our Calling is an unfortunate waste of the talents we've been given. Imagine your entire organization powered by people who have each found their Calling and who are using their finest gifts to serve the world—how extraordinary would your organization be? Or imagine if we all were encouraged and invested in our strengths, so that our inherent or developed mastery became our Calling. Imagine entire teams and organizations comprised of bright, shining, inspiring people whose sparks had all clearly been discovered and ignited. When the spark is glowing, it is unstoppable. As Robert Benchley famously remarked, "It took me fifteen years to discover I had no talent for writing, but I couldn't give it up, because by that time I was too famous."

In developing clarity around your Calling, I invite you to listen to your heart, so that you can follow your passion and thus "hear" where it would guide you in choosing your work. This might lead to radical thinking—perhaps even ending your current work, if it feels like drudgery. At first blush, this might seem dangerous or foolhardy—but how dangerous is it to spend your precious life ignoring your talents, to stifle your passion and your gifts, and to be a wage-slave in a business or occupation that is uninspiring? As Mary Oliver has asked us in her ravishing poem, *The Summer Day*, "Tell me, what is it you plan to do with your one wild and precious life?" Live the answer to this question every day. Life is too precious for a moment to be wasted or a gift to be squandered. Reflect on where your gifts and passion lie, and then pursue them. As Albert Schweitzer reminded us, "Success is not the key to happiness. Happiness is the key to success. If you love what you are doing, you will be successful." It is simply not possible to be inspiring while pursuing work that is uninspiring or deadens the soul. You can't put out that which is not within.

Passion Precedes Profit

You may never have heard of Sandra Boynton, although, if you have ever seen a "*Hippo Birdie 2 Ewes*" card, you know her work. This card has sold 10 million copies, and she has sold half a billion greetings cards altogether, along with tens of millions of books and CDs, which have garnered three gold records and one Grammy nomination. All this is not a job for Sandra Boynton—she doesn't do it for the money—she does it because she loves what she does, and of course, the result is that she makes a lot of money. It often works that way. Says Boynton, "I don't do things differently to be different; I do what works for me. To me, the commodity that we consistently overvalue is money, and what we undervalue is our precious and irreplaceable time. Though, of course, to the extent that money can save you time or make it easier to accomplish things, it's a wonderful thing."

The roots of this thinking may flow from what she describes as an "absurdly happy childhood" in Philadelphia. When she was two years old, Sandra Boynton's parents became Quakers and, as the third of four daughters, she attended Germantown Friends School. There, her father taught English and was Head of the Upper School, and, Boynton says, "the best English teacher I ever had." Boynton attributes much of her "upbeat offbeat" attitude to Germantown Friends' arts-centered curriculum, as well as its thorough integration of the values of pacifism, independent inquiry, and individualism. This feisty spirit was demonstrated during her graduation ceremony at Yale (1974), where she received a *Special Master's Magna* somberly bestowed by Charles Davis, the Master of Calhoun, Boynton's residential college. The graduation audience was unaware that this honor was actually a fiction. Boynton's grade point average did not provide for any degree honor at all, but prior to the ceremony, she had convinced Professor Davis: "My parents are here, so I'd really appreciate it if you could just mumble some Latin after my name."

Which comes first—the Calling or the money? Sandra Boynton has built on her publishing successes by turning her prodigious talents to music, collaborating with Mike Ford, who lives five miles away in rural Connecticut, to produce children's albums. One day, when she was working on the album "Philadelphia Chickens," she mentioned to Mike Ford that Meryl Streep (a fellow Yale alumna and a friend) was the only person she could imagine doing complete justice to the song she had composed called "Nobody Understands Me."

The very next day, who should just drop by her studio but Meryl Streep? Not only did she agree to record the song, but she also suggested that actor Kevin Kline might want to record one, too. He sang "Busybusybusy." Among those who have since recorded with Sandra Boynton are Blues Traveler, Alison Krauss, Steve Lawrence and Eydie Gorme, Sha Na Na, Bobby Vee, Gerry & The Pacemakers, Laura Linney, "Weird Al" Yankovic duetting with Kate Winslet, Neil Sedaka, B.B. King, Patti LuPone, The Bacon Brothers with Mickey Hart, Eric Stoltz, Spin Doctors, Mark Lanegan, Hootie and the Blowfish, Natasha Richardson, Billy J. Kramer, and Davy Jones of The Monkees.

Profit is the daughter of passion and intention.

Here is what a Calling sounds like, in Sandra Boynton's words: "I love what I do, I love the people I work with, I care very much about the value of the work I create, and I don't need more money than I have. This is not revolutionary philosophy.

It's just common sense."

As my friend Marianne Williamson puts it, "Success means we go to sleep at night knowing that our talents and abilities were used in a way that served others."

The Passion of a Calling Trumps Obstacles

We discussed the remarkable life and Character of Evelyn Glennie in the previous Reflection. As one of the most eclectic and innovative musicians in the world, she is constantly redefining the goals and expectations of percussion, and creating performances of such vitality that they almost constitute a new type of performance.

One might expect her to have abandoned her dream of being a musician, given her profound deafness. But, as we discussed previously, not only has she overcome these obstacles, she has used them to change the world—in much the same way that Helen Keller did. Glennie knows her gifts, though they may not have been obvious to others, and has honed them and used them to serve—the definition of a Calling.

As she crusades to "teach the world to listen," she explains: "If we can all feel low-frequency vibrations, why can't we feel higher vibrations? It is my belief that we can; it's just that as the frequency gets higher and our ears become more efficient, they drown out the more subtle sense of 'feeling' the vibrations. I spent a lot of time in my youth (with the help of my school percussion teacher Ron Forbes) refining my ability to detect vibrations. I would stand with my hands against the classroom wall while Ron played notes on the timpani (timpani produce a lot of vibrations). Eventually I managed to distinguish the rough pitch of notes by associating where on my body I felt the sound with the sense of perfect pitch I had before losing my hearing. The low sounds I feel mainly in my legs and feet and high sounds might be particular places on my face, neck and chest."

The reality is, when the passion and fire burn for a Calling—there is nothing that can stand in its way—not even deafness for a musician. Passion trumps obstacles.

What do you love so much that you would not call it work? As Mellody Hobson, President of Chicago-based Ariel Investments, puts it, "I don't draw lines in the sand between work and life. When I'm working, I am living."

Turning Your Passion into Your Calling

I lead two lives. One is dedicated to coaching and mentoring leaders and transforming organizational cultures so they become inspiring places for employees, customers, suppliers, and communities. Thirty of Fortune's Most Admired Companies and 12 of Fortune's Best Companies to Work for in America are our clients. And I speak to audiences all over the world each year.

My other life consists of skiing in the winter and kayaking and mountain biking in the summer. Years ago, when I was the CEO of Manpower Ltd., I employed a salesman called Mike. He weighed 285 pounds, drank 6 pints of beer each day, and played 36 holes of golf for as many days of the week as he could—which was usually at least six. He was an awesome golfer. As his manager, I could not easily organize him, encourage him to follow any kind of structure, submit reports, or make sales calls. In fact, I couldn't put him into a box of any kind. Trying to do so, as I soon learned, was like putting socks on an octopus. But his personal production was extraordinary. Clients would call our office and ask to play a round of golf with Mike, so they could personally renew their contracts with us. Mike had a waiting list of clients wanting to get onto his dance card. Trying to remake Mike was not only pointless, but probably commercially risky as well. I know a genius when I see one, so I supported him in every way I could and set aside my need for conformity and control. He was a fabulous and high-producing asset for our company.

I've skied for well over 50 years all over the world, with some of the best skiers on the planet, and I can handle most any kind of ski terrain. Although I have owned a ski home in the mountains for many years, I have spent too little time there because I have been constantly traveling on behalf of our clients—just like all the other non-Mike-like consultants.

One day, I wondered to myself, why can't I be more like Mike? I teach it—why can't I do it? How could I combine my two lives— my two passions really—into one seamless whole? What I have learned over the years from coaching others (and sometimes we are cobbler's children) is that when I am following my Calling— my passion—and using my best gifts to serve, I become inspiring and am therefore more effective at inspiring others. Yet, far too often, we sigh and say, "Someday, I will do that."

So a few years ago, I decided to practice what I preach by initially offering two- to three-day retreats for leaders in my home 10,000 feet up in the mountains. We call it the Leadership Summit,[8] and we teach leaders how to ski better and how to be more effective leaders. In addition to attending our Leadership Summits, some clients have chosen to bring their entire senior leadership teams to spend time with us in the mountains. These private skiing and consultation events,[9] and the Leadership Summit, are both opportunities to improve technical competence in skiing while growing as a leader—as well as strategizing and exchanging ideas or discussing challenges, and making new personal and professional friends. Skiing is a great metaphor for all these. It combines elements of the personality—personal excellence, competition, physical exercise and conditioning, technical training; and elements of the soul—the sense of oneness, the humility and awe one experiences in the mountains, friendship and interdependence with others, an honoring of the sacred, and

---

[8] See www.secretan.com/leadershipsummit
[9] See www.secretan.com/privateconsulting

a connection to the numinous and larger picture of life. By using the metaphor of skiing, participants leave the experience better skiers and re-energized and re-inspired leaders. Many experience personal transformations that change their lives forever.

In a typical winter, I ski over 100 days. People look at me when I mention this to them and they sigh wistfully, saying, "Oh! How I envy that!" But there are two realities here: 1) This is a choice—I have chosen this format and adapted my life and professional practice in order to embrace my two worlds and passions, and 2) It's not all play. I ski every day, but I work every day, too, and many leaders will work very hard with me—to become more inspirational leaders through skiing. It's not a boondoggle—it is a big personal and organizational stretch—for my guests and for me. Marsha Sinetar wrote a book called *Do What You Love, the Money Will Follow*.[10] The advice is in the title. Life is too short to stifle our creativity—if we identify our passions and blend them into unique and valuable resources, we will develop magical and inspiring opportunities to serve and prosper. Funny thing, my dance card now looks a lot like Mike's!

Defining Our Calling

When Al Gore was running for president of the United States, he was following a path—perhaps one that met the needs of his social self. The pain of the Florida debacle marked the end of his 2000 election campaign, and he became only the fourth person in United States history to win the popular vote but lose a presidential election—in this case to George W. Bush. He retreated to his home and reflected. With encouragement from his wife, Tipper Gore, he began to build on his real passion—the decline of Earth's environment (his Terrathreat)—and to build a compelling message detailing what he calls "the most serious crisis we've

---

[10] Dell; Other Printing edition, 1989

ever faced." This passion eclipsed his earlier passion for politics, giving him, as *Time* magazine put it, "...freer rein to matters of the heart and spirit than he ever could as a candidate."

Says his wife, Tipper, "He's got access to every leader in every country, the business community, people of every political stripe. He can do this his way, all over the world, for as long as he wants. That's freedom. Why would anyone give that up?"

Says Al Gore, "There's no question I'm freed up. I don't want to suggest that it's impossible to be free and authentic within the political process, but it's obviously harder. Another person might be better at it than I was... And now it is easier for me to just let it fly."

Al Gore has trained thousands to broadcast his message; he has won an Oscar for his movie *An Inconvenient Truth* and received the Nobel Prize. According to Tipper, Al Gore is "now more comfortable with who he is, he is doing what he is most passionate about, that's why it's working."

It always works that way. Following our true Calling frees up our deepest gifts, thus creating the opportunity for us to serve at our best—and at the highest level.

When we define our Calling, we are describing how we plan to use our (natural and acquired) gifts and talents to serve. If we first define and then use our gifts and talents to serve others and the world, we will live lives that are inspiring to us and to others, and we will align our lives with our Destiny and our Character.

Rob Ryder, Vice President of Learning and Leadership Development at Centura Health, describes his Calling this way: *To awaken souls to the beauty they can create, through my writing, teaching, speaking and musicianship.*

Rob is responsible for encouraging and supporting the personal growth of the leaders of a 14,000-employee organization. He and his team direct all training, learning, and curriculum development for all of the organization's leaders. He describes how defining his Destiny, Character, and Calling Statements guided his work and life: "For me, putting my Character into words brought together my hopes and dreams with intentions and possibility. My Character Statement definitely describes the journey and not the destination. However, the Character Statement makes the possibility of multiple destinations clear. At the moment, I am called to live into my Character through my Callings of leadership, composing, directing, and performing music, and public speaking and presenting. As I learn and grow with time, my Calling(s) may change to reflect new skills, interests, and intellectual and physical pursuits. I believe, however, that my Callings will always be focused and guided by my Character, which defines the essence of who I am and will not change. My Destiny will be defined by the way I touch others and am touched by others as I live into my Character. The Character exists in one's heart, whether it is memorialized in writing or not. Writing it down provides a concrete acknowledgment to one's self of the direction, possibility, and goodness within."

We can each be inspired by more than one Calling. Rob Ryder is inspired by leading and helping others to grow, directing and composing music, and presenting his ideas to audiences. I love to teach leadership, to inspire organizations, and to write. I am also a professional skier and an accredited ski instructor and a passionate kayaker and mountain biker. Like Rob Ryder, I blend all these different loves into one seamless life.

The great Persian poet Rumi wrote:

There is one thing in this world that you must never forget to do. If you forget everything else and not this, there's nothing to worry about, but if you remember everything else, and forget this, then you will have done nothing in your life.

It's as if a king has sent you to some country to do a task, and you perform a hundred other services, but not the one he sent you to do. So human beings come to this world to do particular work. That work is the purpose, and each is

*specific to the person. If you don't do it, it's as though a
priceless Indian sword were used to slice rotten meat. It's a
golden bowl being used to cook turnips, when one filing
from the bowl could buy a hundred suitable pots. It's a
knife of the finest tempering nailed into a wall to hang
things on.*

*You say, "But look, I'm using the dagger. It's not lying
idle." Do you hear how ludicrous that sounds? For a penny,
an iron nail could be bought to serve the purpose. You say,
"But I spend my energies on lofty enterprises. I study
jurisprudence and philosophy and logic and astronomy
and medicine and all the rest." But consider why you do
those things. They are all branches of yourself.*

*Remember the deep root of your being, the presence of
your lord. Give your life to the one who already owns your
breath and your moments. If you don't, you will be exactly
like the man who takes a precious dagger and hammers it
into his kitchen wall for a peg to hold his dipper gourd.
You'll be wasting valuable keenness and foolishly
ignoring your dignity and your purpose.*

The first question then, is, "What do you truly love?" By this
I mean, what is it that truly calls to you, that deep down, at a
visceral level, you love to do, because you find it exhilarating and
profoundly inspiring? What enchants you? What romances you?
What creates magic in your life? What career path do you secretly
wish you had chosen years ago? Do you see yourself as a "could-
have/should-have-been" rock star, trial lawyer, jet pilot, neuro-
surgeon, forest ranger, or firefighter? What are your true gifts?
Did you choose a career that met the needs of your social self but
left your essential self unfulfilled—did you forsake your North
Star? When you dream about a life that is the one that slipped by
you—do you wistfully yearn for the clock to be turned back so
that you could start over? If so, remember, it's never too late.

St. Francis, the son of a prosperous merchant, took part in several military operations as a mercenary soldier before he felt himself called to be a preacher and mystic at the age of 27. He founded two holy orders in the last third of his life, dying when he was forty-five. Bill Wilson was 40 before he started the organization that would change the lives of millions—Alcoholics Anonymous. Rosa Parks was 42 when she signaled the beginning of the end of segregation and ushered in a new phase of the civil rights movement by refusing to give up her seat to a white passenger on a bus. Golda Meir became Prime Minister of Israel at 71. Grandma Moses *began* painting when she was 80, completed 1,500 painting after that, and 25 percent of her paintings were completed after she was 100 years old! *It's never too late to rediscover your true Calling.*

Think of your true Calling as inhaling the memory of virtuosity not yet experienced.

I am reminded of the words of my friend Debbie Ford: "Your mind can't take you where your heart longs to go." In the spaces below, write down those things that your heart is calling you to do and that you are gifted at doing—regardless of whether you do them now or not—those things that, if you had complete freedom, you would spend the rest of your life learning and doing. Listen to your heart here, and try to ignore the editing voice that issues from your mind:

The true gifts (or skills) to which my heart is called are:

_____

_____

Perhaps you are inspired and enchanted by the path that you have already chosen and simply wish that it contained more ginger, more zing, more excitement, and fulfillment? There is nothing wrong with being in love with what you do—indeed you are fortunate to feel this way—so how would you add more inspiration, passion, love, and exhilaration to what you do now? How would you ignite your spark?

The work I do today needs more:

_____

_____

As you reflect on these thoughts, try to reveal within them the gifts that have been suppressed, overlooked, or forgotten. As Leo Buscaglia said, "Our talents are the gift that God gives to us...What we make of our talents is our gift back to God." Until our true talents and gifts are rediscovered, polished, and honed, and then offered in service to others, we will remain a shadow of our potential.

What are those secret longings for you? What—if you were to operate at your personal best—would you be doing with your precious life? What do you care about so much that you would *pay to do it*? If you won the lottery, what would you do? What livelihood would you pursue if you were being guided solely by your essential self, with no constraints being applied by the social self? What work draws perfectly on your talent and fuels your passion? What work rises out of a great need in the world, flowing from your essential self, that you feel drawn to meet? This is where you will find your Calling, your voice, the fullness of your North Star. This is where your gifts and talents intersect with your passion and the needs of the world. As Fred Buechner wrote, "The place God calls you to, is the place where your deep gladness and the world's deep hunger meet."

Let's return to Shirley Willihnganz to see how she developed her Calling Statement. As you will recall, Shirley's Destiny is, "To create a more joyful world," and her Character Statement is, "To be a hopeful and joyful person." What is important to Shirley is her desire to "connect others to what they love." She also longs to create closeness among people. She's good at it, too. She says, "My strengths, I've been told, include a wide latitude of accept-ance, empathy, transparency, a great ability to accommodate sit-uations or others, good communication and interpersonal skills, imagination, an ability to listen and understand, synthesize and incorporate data (although I'm not especially data driven), even-tempered and, in my boss's words, "a steady center when every-thing is falling apart." Maybe all that does suggest that I'm here to connect others to what they love." And so Shirley settled on this Calling Statement:

To inspire others to do what they love through leadership, service, teaching and speaking

Imagine working for someone who you know is passionate about inspiring you to do what you love, a leader who is living and leading from her essential self. This is how leaders become inspiring for those they lead and serve.

The livelihood that would best serve my essential self is:

_____

_____

The next question for you to answer is this: "What must I do to ensure that the intersection of my talents and passion serves the needs of the world, and thus guides my current path?"

_____

_____

Developing Your Own Personal Calling Statement

Here are some examples of Personal Calling Statements that may stir your creative juices:

To mentor, partner and walk with others on their journey to wholeness
Sister Nancy Hoffman, former VP of Mission, Centura Health

To serve others through sacred writing and communication
Simone Gabbay, author and editor

To serve leaders to uncover their greatness through my coaching, facilitation and writing
Ron Mandel, Secretan Center Faculty Member

To provide visionary, transformational leadership in healthcare
Mike McCallister, President and CEO, Humana Inc.

To teach, coach and model the integration of spirit and performance
Ken Jacobsen, Secretan Center Faculty Member

And my own:
To lead and serve others through writing, teaching, and speaking

By putting these three steps together—Destiny, Character, and Calling—we bring clarity to who we are. It affirms **Why** we are here, how we will **Be**, and what we will **Do** during our visit to this planet. So we call these three combined statements our **Why-Be-Do.** Our Why-Be-Do becomes our North Star. By gaining this inner clarity (a rare achievement only attained by a few), we are able to move our lives forward with uncommon focus and passion. As a result, we re-inspire ourselves and renew our capacity for inspiring others. This is our spark.[11]

Here is a complete Why-Be-Do from Robin Mooney, Sales Executive at Herman Miller:

Destiny: To inspire brilliance
Character: To live with love, joy and passion
Calling: To lead courageously with love, authenticity and inspiration

What is your Calling Statement?

_____

_____

_____

First say to yourself what you would be; and then do what you have to do.

Epictetus

---

[11] Submit your own Why-Be-Do Statement and draw inspiration from reading those of many others at www.secretan.com/whybedo.

Reflection Four: 5 DYNAMICS

I have to go. I'm conducting a seminar in multiple personality disorders, and it takes me forever to fill out the nametags.

Niles Crane (David Hyde Pierce)

We ignite the spark within us through relationships and understanding ourselves and each other better. Why we are here, how we want to be in our lives, and how we wish to serve—our *Why-Be-Do*—these are the questions that have tantalized humans for eons. If we could find an instrument that helps us understand ourselves better and how we can relate with others and the world more effectively, we would have a precious aid at our disposal. There is just such a tool.

A Short History of Personality-Based Assessment Tools

The most widely used psychometric profiling systems in corporations today rely on the original work of Carl Jung (1875-1961). These instruments, as well as others that draw from different personality-based theories, have long been the major influence guiding corporate managers who seek the holy grail of personality definition. They ceaselessly quest for this because they believe that understanding how to identify, manipulate, and control the behavior of employees and customers will yield higher performance and improved results. Modern human resources and leadership theory and policy rely heavily on this wide but sometimes shallow vein of personality-based tools. Research shows that at best they are a crude measure which, beyond the obvious advantage of at least putting the subject on management's radar, yields very few meaningful insights that enhance leadership development or performance. As Edward de Bono said, "You can't dig a hole in a different place by digging the same hole deeper." Our constant search in the field of Jungian psychology for pat solutions to the mystery we call a human, may have reached its useful limits, and the reason for our search—to manipulate and control behavior—is also pointless. We are like ancient alchemists, searching the desert for the philosopher's stone in order to find the panacea —wrong place, wrong theory, wrong motivation.

Another disadvantage of working with personality is that people make many attributions to "personality" without any clear agreement on what personality is. Researchers such as Gordon Allport have found 50 definitions of personality. Nonetheless, focusing on personality certainly remains the dominant method used today for understanding people at work and in life. While personality can offer valuable insights, it can be a difficult concept with which to work. There is little that seems to be bound up more closely with an individual than his or her personality. As Norman O. Brown said, "I am what is mine. Personality is the original personal property." People assume it to be immutable, and much more difficult to change than, say, behavior. Self-image and self-worth are often intrinsically bound up in one's perception of personality. Cognitive and perceptual phenomena are often misattributed to personality. The jargon of personality is highly specialized and may be unfamiliar to, or misused by, people who apply personality theory to making professional judgments in the workplace.

In many ways, the preoccupation with personality is a set of blinders, a distraction, and an illusion that separates us from other people and ourselves—accentuating separateness rather than guiding us intelligently to our goal of oneness. Interacting with people on the basis of mutual energies is much healthier than trying to figure out personality and restricting ourselves to living in the realm of the social self.

Energy Focus

An alternative is to consider the concept of "energy focus." Energy has been well understood, and indeed is a dominant part of almost every culture, on every continent and in every epoch—*except* for North America in the 20th and 21st centuries! In China, for example, energetically based acupuncture is ubiquitous, as is the concept of *qi*, loosely defined as "energy flow." The management of this energy forms the basis of Traditional Chinese Medicine. Focused energy is central to Buddhist beliefs, where it is called *prana*. In India, the practice of yoga is based on an energetic linkage between physical routines and meditation, with the effects on the brain's alpha and beta waves having been indisputably measured by countless electroencephalograms (EEGs).

In the United States, Mihaly Csikszentmihalyi, Distinguished Professor of Psychology at Claremont Graduate University, has documented a neurological phenomenon which he calls "flow state." He acknowledges that it shares a great deal with Taoist and Zen Buddhist concepts, which have endured through thousands of years. Highly evolved practitioners of such knowledge systems subject them to standards and controls that are different from those applied by the more recent Western science. Extensive research has shown that meditative states provide different outputs on EEGs. How and why this happens is still unknown—and to the Easterner's way of thinking, which more readily embraces the mysterious, it is also likely to be of less concern.

However, the construct of energy need not belong only to Eastern culture. Robert Quinn and Jane Dutton of the University of Michigan Business School define energy as "a type of positive affective arousal, which people can experience as emotion—short responses to specific events—or mood, longer lasting affective states that need not be a response to a specific event." Martin Seligman of the University of Pennsylvania has been developing these concepts under the aegis of "Positive Psychology." The concept of "energy" is becoming part of mainstream thinking because it is instantly self-identifiable, indeed universal, and therefore an essential part of an inspiring leader's journey to becoming more inspired and inspiring.

To be an inspiring leader, we do not need to emphasize the external. Instead, we need to *practice* the internal. In other words, if we understand ourselves, and if we understand our energy preferences, we will be able to use them to inspire *all* people—not just some, and not just because we want to manipulate them. We are not trying to *do* something to others; we are trying to *be* something that inspires others, sharing the *realness* of who we are, instead of the persona behind which we so often hide. Being an inspiring leader rests on this essential distinction. Failure to understand it will keep us stuck in an old and unproductive model, while understanding and living this difference can move us towards breakthroughs in our effectiveness as leaders—so that we can change the world.

We all have energies that we bring to the task at hand, whether it is sending an e-mail, making love, saving the world, building a kitchen cabinet, driving a car, or raising children. Those energies are innate and spring from a deep place—from our essential self—our soul. Who we are can be defined by the ratio of four energies and their relationship to each other. The four energies are called *Explore, Excite, Examine,* and *Execute.* Michael Sturm, the creator of the 5 Dynamics model, defined these energies after observing distinctive preferences in how individuals approached certain tasks and processes. They are called "energies" because they help us to move through the cycle of anything we wish to achieve, from the original conception or inspiration to the end result. While these four energies are not immutable, the ratio of one to the other is unlikely to change much during our lifetime—barring a traumatic change to our essential selves.

What happens next? These four lead us to a fifth "place"—the phase during which we *Evaluate*. This is not quite an energy, but rather a way of considering how all the preceding and associated causal energies occurred, and how we might better interact with the world, and with ourselves, the next time around the cycle. When we arrive at the *Evaluate* part of the cycle, we are able to measure whether we have met the needs of our social self (our personality), defined as *success*, and the needs of our *essential self* (our soul), defined as *satisfaction* or *joy*.

The cycle of the four energies of 5 Dynamics can be visually depicted in this way:

Energies and Learning Styles

More than forty-five years ago, W. Michael Sturm began to integrate many of the leading personality tests of the time and bring the various theories to the process of how people learn, which had been his lifelong passion. He began observing the patterns of test-takers when he administered instruments to them, and he methodically mapped out the process that the student applied to complete the test. Over time, he began to see patterns in these behaviors, as well as correlations between the patterns and the test outcomes. However, the *process* often delivered more information than the test score. For example, children approach tasks in a particular way based not on what they have learned, but on how they naturally go about doing things. He also observed the same phenomenon with adults.

Sturm was able to look at testing in an unusual way because he approached it as a social psychologist rather than as a clinical counseling psychologist. The difference is critical: Clinical psychologists test X to measure X. Social psychologists put people in situations where they think they are doing X, but they are really doing Y. To social psychologists, the ultimate score isn't nearly as important as watching the *process* of the person undertaking the experiment. And this led Mike Sturm to realize that process was more important than outcome—*how* we do things, rather than *what* we do—because the energy favored by an individual will determine the process they choose to complete any given task. The majority of people's lives are not spent in outcomes, but in the journey toward achieving them. Observations of these journeys, or processes, therefore yield much more information than ultimate outcomes or scores. In part as a consequence of this belief, the 5 Dynamics tools became process-based: they examine how a person works, not just what his or her ultimate output might be.

Sturm also became involved with the Quaker movement in Boston and Cambridge. The Quakers put great emphasis on

The four energies can be described like this:

5 Dynamics Inc. ENERGY INTENSITY FLOWS

Exploring	Exciting	Examining	Executing
HOW SHE OR HE PERCEIVES THE WORLD:			
Wants to know "How?"	Wants to know "Who"	Wants to know "Why?"	Wants to know "What?"
Prefers to "live in the future"	Prefers to "live in the now"	Prefers the past	Prefers immediate measurable time-frames
High interest in creative and visionary thinking, metaphors, concepts, causes, and people	High interest in people and places	High interest in details and facts backed by hard data	High interest in action and objects
Intuitive, non-linear, and independent thinking	Spontaneous and intuitive jazz-like improvisation	Intense ability to focus; thinking is rigorous and thorough	Concrete pragmatic thinking, common sense — limited options and traditional approaches
Seeks wholeness and unity	Seeks synergy through interaction and play	Seeks "truth" through validation of data	Seeks results through challenge, competition, and confrontation
Able to see patterns and connections	Strong interpersonal relater, works through stories and inspiration	Sees world through logic, facts, and data. "What has worked well in the past?"	Understands concrete, pragmatic ideas
Considers all options, feelings, and reasons; dedicated	Charming and adaptable; a "people" person	Seemingly distant or impersonal; dead-pan expression; not outwardly oral but listens acutely	Enacting, moving, and driving
Idealist; anti-authoritarian	Persuasive optimist	Skeptic	Authoritative

Exploring	Exciting	Examining	Executing
THEIR ENERGY INTENSITY <u>INCREASES</u> WHEN THEY MUST:			
Deepen understanding of possibilities and potential	Raise energy and gather power	Create competence and confidence through due diligence	Get it done!
Broaden the scope	Acknowledge strengths and capacities of others	Promote safety and rigor	Direct power
Align all functions to the mission	Inject fun	Study what's possible or impossible with data	Lead and shape groups
Promote inclusivity, unity, and coherence	Invite healthy and productive interactions	Justify rules, procedures, and timelines	Challenge and activate; push hard for results
Promote health and wellness	Advocate fairness	Perform "reality" checks	Demand action and accountability
THEIR ENERGY INTENSITY <u>DECREASES</u> WHEN THEY MUST:			
Deal with limitations, rules, and restrictions	Ignore distractions	Deal with the feeling of being rushed or pushed	See the ideal
Complete things immediately	Contain their impulsivity	Show more flexibility over prolonged periods	Deal with optional thinking
Deal with conflict	Stay disciplined	Outwardly demonstrate passion and personal concern	Tolerate too many options
Resist the urge to over-commit	Work alone, or cannot delegate to others	Take risks	Resist the urge to take command of the outcome
Take decisive actions over prolonged periods	Express things in only a few words	See patterns and the big picture	Demonstrate patience over prolonged periods
Make tough decisions, prioritize, or say "no"	Take time before committing to a task	Not sweat the small stuff	Share control
Be fully "present"	Accept more responsibility over prolonged periods	Envision an optimistic future	Slow down
Set firm and consistent interpersonal boundaries	Know when to get serious	Recognize internal states and needs of self and others	Open up, lighten up, loosen up
Resist the urge to take things personally	Stay out of the spotlight	Let go and move on	Put people-concerns first and results second

"active witnessing," which involves simultaneous external and internal focus. This practice subsequently became useful in the development of the 5 Dynamics assessment; by watching thousands of people take assessments, Sturm observed that most people's attention broke between the 24th and 28th items. It became Sturm's goal, therefore, to reduce the number of items in any test to 24 or less. This work culminated in a lead article in the *Journal of Social Psychology* under the name of Richard Sprinthall, who was Sturm's faculty advisor.

During the 1970s and 1980s, Sturm became a differential diagnostician for learning preferences. The prevailing belief at the time was that children who performed poorly in school were either brain damaged or learning disabled. Sturm again took a contrarian view: they were *learning different* and likely *brain different*. He found that if he understood a child's learning process, and matched it to a teacher with a similar process, and also helped the parents adapt to the process, the results were remarkably successful. His theory and its practical applications became more pronounced when he became a psychoeducational consultant to a mental health center in Northern Maine and a director of special education for two school districts in the State. He and his colleagues began developing integrative reading, writing, and math programs that raised the achievement levels of special education and Chapter One[12] students by 3.5 years during a 3-year period.

This led to another breakthrough discovery: If we understand how people learn, we can connect to them much more effectively. So, when we add these components together—being aware of our own energy, learning style, and process preferences, understanding the same in others, and marrying these in service of the whole, we create awareness of the essential self, or soul, and thus

---

[12] Children with disabilities whose education is financially supported by government funds

inspiration for the other person and for ourselves—and this results in inspiring leadership.

It is somewhat unusual for the National Science Foundation (NSF) to study the impact of a psychometric instrument, but they recently did so because they were deeply impressed with the documented, "remarkable" outcomes at a community college program for high-risk and at-risk students. The NSF found that students in the 5 Dynamics program on average enjoyed the following success rates compared to the control groups:

- Grade-point average improved by 80 percent
- Units completed per term improved by 76 percent
- Persistence (the ratio of the number of terms students who attempted coursework, regardless of grades, to the number of consecutive pairs of semesters) improved by 82 percent

Imagine being able to achieve increases of this order in the performance levels of employees within your own organization!

This last finding suggested not just an increase in cognitive abilities, but also a deep fundamental shift in the students' perception of self-worth, as well as their ability to collaborate with peers to achieve a common goal. In other words, if we can understand the learning styles of others—their energy preferences— they will be inspired. It is not something we do to them; it is the heightened awareness of our own energy preferences, coupled with a heightened awareness of the energy preferences of others, that connects us as one, and is therefore inspiring to others. In other words, unlike so many alternative theories, our self-awareness has the effect of altering the behavior of others, much like the *Heisenberg Effect*, named after German Nobel-laureate physicist Werner Karl Heisenberg (1901-1976), whose uncertainty principle states that (in particle physics experiments) the very act of observing alters the position of the particle being observed. And the remarkable results that occur reflect back on us because the inspiration experienced by others causes us to be even more inspired. This creates a virtuous circle—the more our way of being with them aligns with the inspiring qualities embodied in our Character Statement, the more others will be inspired, and therefore the more our own level of inspiration will be raised. As James M. Barrie put it, "Those who bring sunshine into the lives of others, cannot keep it from themselves." And so a self-reinforcing pattern of inspiration begins.

I have used the 5 Dynamics tool in many organizations and have always been astounded by the way it is received. Typically people will say, "How could you get so much accurate information from so few questions?" and, "This is the most accurate profile I have ever seen." A great benefit of 5 Dynamics is what are called "dyads." These are reports that describe how one person can most effectively relate with another—how we can best inspire them—in other words, become one with them, a fusion of our respective energies. This informs us about how best to connect our essential self to that of another—so that our interaction is not based on personality, which is so often our default behavior and also the most common guidance from many psychometric profiles.

Dyads can be created for those relating to each other as, for example, leader to employee, peer to peer, coach to coachee, parent to child, spouse to spouse, or friend to friend. Through this process, individuals gain a new awareness of their energy preferences, as well as those of others, and are therefore able to achieve a remarkable breakthrough in their relational skills. I have seen entire teams recalibrate their relationships and move to an entirely new level of performance in just a matter of days.

What this remarkable instrument can do is shine a light into our essential selves in a way that no other instrument I know of is capable of doing. This inner awareness is one of the foundational steps in becoming the inspiring person who is able to lead others in a way that inspires them. It is one of the ways we ignite the spark to light the flame that can light a torch.

With each copy of this book, you are entitled to one free personal copy of your own *5 Dynamics eXpress Report*. This is an abridged version of the more comprehensive 5 Dynamics Assessment that is available from **www.secretan.com/5dynamics**. To obtain your profile, and learn more about 5 Dynamics, visit **www.secretan.com/5d** to receive your unique user name and password.

You must stop this interview now as I have come to the end of my personality.

Quentin Crisp

Reflection Five: THE ONE DREAM

There is nothing like a dream to create the future.
Victor Hugo

Over thirty years of working with leading organizations, I have learned that the common, unifying experience among winning teams, great endeavors, and extraordinary achievements— is a dream. A dream lights our spark. Even more powerful is the fact that a dream can light the spark for an entire organization. A dream represents the uniqueness that can be found in groups of people who achieve the extraordinary—creating revolutions, overthrowing despots, founding religions or nations (or fusing them into one), climbing Everest, reinventing organizations, creating breakthroughs, building something extraordinary, or changing the way we live or think or how the world works. It is true of organizations, sports teams, film crews, orchestras, states, cities, countries—even families.

Over the last 50 years of business theorizing and academic and professional development, we have succeeded in expanding our capacity to quantify, measure, and analyze, but we have stifled our capacity to dream. It has become conventional thinking that dreaming is too "out there" for a business environment. As a result, we shy away from talking about dreams in organizations. Instead, we have created "mission, vision, and values" statements. But the currency of mission, vision, and values statements has been devalued, their indiscriminate use and homogeneity rendering them feeble, uninspiring, and indistinguishable from everyone else's. The stale barrenness of mission, vision, or values statements pales in comparison to the inspiring power and passion that are embedded in a dream. In fact, many organizations have reduced the process of developing a personal mission into a banal, multiple-choice exercise—three columns, choose one word from each. Even Dilbert was offering advice on building mission statements for a while!

Leadership and Big Dreams

The role of the leader is to inspire by identifying, realizing, and sustaining a dream.

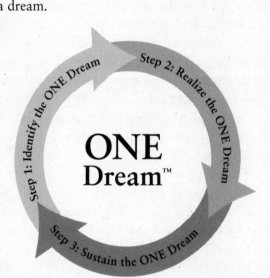

What we are really discussing here is passion and how organizations can ignite a similar and necessary spark of excitement and energy in their colleagues and customers that will fuel the accomplishment of something extraordinary—such as a dream. Not a five-percent increase in market share or a ten-percent return on equity—but a bold, daring, impudent, audacious, outrageous, thrilling, exhilarating, and inspiring dream.

How did we land a man on the moon? The Russians had just successfully launched *Sputnik*, effectively winning the space race, and Americans were in a funk. John F. Kennedy's solution was to define a dream, and it was a dream so powerful that thousands of people embraced it, made it their own, and thus made it real. Indeed, it was such a powerful dream that it restored America's self-esteem, galvanized Americans, and inspired much of the rest of the world. Dreams are like that; they transcend differences, disagreements, and petty arguments, because the dream unifies us at a higher level, engages us in a higher purpose, and fuses us— as ONE. "Galvanize" is an important word here: while we may all have our opinions and even our disagreements, a dream occupies territory that is above these differences, and therefore it has a galvanizing effect on a group of people while leaving their differences intact. It achieves oneness at the highest level, *and* it *includes* the diversity of ideas and beliefs. And it is this elusive oneness—which, when achieved, is the highest form of inspiration—for which we are yearning. Dreams are almost unique in their power to inspire through achieving oneness. A team that shares a dream is ONE.

We have worked with many organizations where the internal competition for resources, ideology, and the need for control or power have hampered the development of a unified vision. The creation of what we have come to call ONE Dream raises the aspirations of all the parties—inspiring them as ONE—because a dream elevates the conversation to Higher Ground, above the mundane and the pedestrian, to where the inspiration of shared ideals hold sway, leaving the squabbles over territory, power, and position to the lower ground.

Great historical leaders—Christ, Buddha, Lao-Tzu, Confucius, Mohammed, Nelson Mandela, Mother Teresa, and Martin Luther King, Jr. among them—all had a dream. In his famous speech delivered on the steps of the Lincoln Memorial in Washington, D.C., on August 28, 1963, Martin Luther King, Jr. repeated

"I have a dream..." eight times. It was his ability to articulate his dream that united thousands of people and inspired them to usher in a new era of civil rights and liberties. And that dream continues to inspire today.

Dreams are like that—they have the power within them to change the world. And great dreams, carefully executed, are sustainable.

In order to unlock the potential and power of modern leadership to transform clients, organizations, communities, cities, and countries or the world, we must understand and harness the power of the dream.

The ONE Dream for Organizations

In coaching and guiding leaders of organizations around the world, we've noticed that our work with Higher Ground Leadership has resulted in amazing outcomes. In fact, in the foreword to my book *Inspire! What Great Leaders Do*, 15 CEOs and senior executives wrote:

> *The principles of Higher Ground Leadership have helped our organizations reduce staff turnover by as much as 66 percent, double levels of employee morale and patient and customer satisfaction, increase the clinical outcomes of many procedures, implement Six Sigma programs successfully, thus contributing to dramatic cost savings and waste elimination, cut the time taken to prepare operating rooms by 50 percent and dramatically increase their throughput, increase profits by 1,000 percent and eliminate layoffs and the use of outsourced labor. Higher Ground Leadership touches the whole human, not just the working human, so it has helped to heal marriages, improve relationships between parents and children, among others, contributed to addiction cessation, strengthened values and beliefs, and raised personal*

performance. Most importantly, it has contributed to personal fulfillment, meaning, and inspiration and, therefore, organizational performance and reputation. One person stated simply that, after the birth of her children, Higher Ground Leadership was the most important experience in her life.

When leaders are invited to describe their richly imagined ONE Dream for the organization, remarkable things happen: they focus on aspirations that are not the usual corporate vanilla statements, and they describe their most extraordinary, outrageous, never-before-achieved hopes, often secretly held until then, because they now have permission to be fearless and imaginative, to think outside the box, and to be truly outrageous and unusually creative. Leaders come up with some remarkable ideas—hospitals who dream of eliminating all avoidable deaths, banks who dream of changing the world, corporations who dream of becoming environmentally friendly, regional communities who dream of becoming world-class centers of excellence and innovation, organizations who dream of a richly imagined future—and these are all from our direct client experiences.

ONE Dream for Louisville

For example, the ONE Dream which we helped create for the Louisville, Kentucky/Southern Indiana, region, is:

The Idea Capital of the World: Where Imaginations and Individuals Thrive

Louisville thinks of itself as a place where dreams get introduced to a "can-do" spirit, where the people share a belief in the creative power of opportunity, expression, and imagination. Alive with potential and inspired by a progressive spirit of possibility and aspiration, Louisville is a special place—somewhere between "way out there" and "feels like home."

The spirit of what is possible in Louisville is exemplified by those things for which it is famous: the Kentucky Derby, the Muhammad Ali Center, whose mission is to foster peace and mediation, the Louisville Slugger, and by those things that remain under the radar and provide a sense of surprise and discovery for the first-time visitor: the number one hotel in America according to *Conde Naste*, more restaurants per capita than any other American city, and the amazing Bourbon Trail, which unites the rural "bourbon makers" with the cosmopolitan "bourbon drinkers" of the world.

The region is birthplace to ideas that have changed the world—those of Abraham Lincoln, Harlan Sanders, James Audubon, and Diane Sawyer. It is home to research that developed the first cancer vaccine, first successful hand transplant, and first artificial heart transplant. And it is creating a beautiful future for the next 50 years by funding the largest urban parks initiative in North America. The region blends the best of two states, 186 cities and towns, two metropolitan areas, and numerous rural and urban neighborhoods. It is a place that truly wants to set an example for others by ensuring that everyone, including those who are less fortunate, has an opportunity to thrive. This dream serves as inspiration to the one-and-a-half million individuals who live there and the future generations to come.

ONE Dream for ATB Financial

ATB Financial (ATB) is a full-service financial institution headquartered in Edmonton, Alberta, Canada. It is the largest Alberta-based financial institution, with assets of $26.5 billion, more than 5,000 employees serving 670,000 Albertans in 244 communities through 164 branches and 133 agencies, a Customer Contact Centre, a network of Automated Banking Machines (ABMs) across

Alberta, as well as Internet and telephone services. ATB was established in 1938 and has been owned by the provincial government since 1997. It has been named one of Canada's 50 Best Employers by *Report on Business* magazine, one of the 75 Best Workplaces in Canada by the Great Place to Work Institute, and one of Alberta's Top 40 Employers by Mediacorp Canada Inc.

With the arrival of a new CEO, Dave Mowat, the company decided to review its history, explore its horizons, and define its legacy. What Dave and his leadership team understood so well was that the image of banking wasn't always positive, and the methodologies of "mission, vision, and values" were tired and boring, and they recognized the need to refresh and inspire the company's morale and presence in the market.

We were invited to be advisors for ATB, and our research revealed by the strategic map we prepared showed that Albertans would support and encourage a financial institution that

1. has the ability to *get to the heart of the matter*, to cut to the chase, and know what is important and necessary;
2. is willing to take action—to be a catalyst who instigates growth and expansion, by
3. providing brilliantly simple ideas and solutions that *get to the heart of the matter*.

This is an endless and self-reinforcing loop, which, if met by ATB's employees, will win the hearts and minds of customers.

From this, ATB reflected on their strengths and values—what was most important to them and how they could best serve their employees and customers in a distinctive way. Three key points emerged that spoke to their essence:

1. Changing the world and making it a better place—being a significant, positive force in the lives of others
2. Putting people first—not profits—in the belief that this

priority, well executed, always accomplishes the profit objectives

3. Helping farmers, business people, entrepreneurs, families, young people, employees—everyone—to make their dreams come true

And so the ONE Dream for ATB became:

"Changing Our World by Putting People First and Making Their Dreams Come True"

Realizing the ONE Dream means making sure that *everyone* lives it. In banking, the controls and hurdles for obtaining credit are significant, and it is often easier for a banker to say "no" than it is to work out a solution that meets the needs of a potential borrower. But saying "no" doesn't change the world, nor does it put people first or help this customer's dreams come true. Clearly, the right answer for achieving these ONE Dream aspirations at ATB would be to say "yes"—but how is this best achieved?

Nolan Berg, ATB's vice-president of Marketing, tells the story of a branch manager who was approached by a young man just two weeks into his first job. The young man had no credit rating, no references or previous employment, and he wanted to buy a used car. The manager said, "Given your background and lack of credit history, most bankers would tell you 'no.'" After explaining ATB's ONE Dream, he continued, "But I am going to tell you 'yes.' Here is what I want you to do: I am going to give you a credit card. I want you to use it and to pay off your account promptly each month when it is due. If you do this for six months, come back and see me, and I will lend you the money to buy your car."

Realizing the ONE Dream of ATB could not be achieved with a "no"; it needed a "yes" accompanied by a creative, compassionate heart.

These are not the kinds of creative and exciting aspirations or transformational changes in culture that fit easily under a monotonous heading of "mission, vision, and values." Gary Ridge, president and CEO of WD-40 Company, has shown his disdain for mission statements by offering this spoof version, "WD-40 will create positive lasting memories by stopping squeaks, getting rid of smells and getting rid of dirt."

A much larger canvas is needed for painting magnificent ideas—they require a dream.

We invite leaders to believe in the dream, to trust that the dream is realizable and that when the energies of their entire organization are harnessed behind that dream, it will be achieved. An organization with 10,000 employees that harnesses the passion—the total energy of every employee (and vendor, customer, union member, regulator, media, and others)—behind that dream begins a journey towards a previously unattained level of performance.

Finding the "Music" as well as the Words for the ONE Dream

A dream cannot simply be pulled out of thin air, or the "gut" of an individual or a group of executives. A dream must rest on the structure of a rigorous platform. The precision of sound research is required in order to validate the feasibility of a dream and confirm that the required propelling forces are available for its attainment.

But conventional research has a dismal track record. Extremely few researchers, including few of the best brains on the planet, were able to predict the financial meltdown of 2008—they simply didn't see it coming, even with their widespread use of renowned research techniques. Seventy percent of new products fail, despite the billions of research dollars invested every year by some of the best organizations in the world. We have developed a brilliant understanding and application of mathematics, but we haven't figured out what the mathematics should measure. In employee satisfaction surveys, if an employee is asked, "Does your supervisor, or someone at work, seem to care about you as a person?" (a standard question in the Gallup Q12 Survey), the answer will depend on any number of variables: for example, on whether I crashed my car coming in to work this morning, or if my husband told me he was leaving me last night, or if I just received a raise or a promotion, or if I just learned I have a terminal illness. In other words, the subconscious mood will influence the conscious data and skew the resulting data collected. If we then apply sophisticated analyses to the aggregate of this flawed data and implement far-reaching strategies based on our interpretations of those analyses, we can find ourselves hopelessly off course. We may have some measure of the words, but we keep overlooking the importance of the music.

When the French movie-theme composer Maurice Jarre added his music into movies, it had much the same effect as adding water to sulfuric acid—it boiled. Jarre earned three Academy Awards—for *Lawrence of Arabia* (1962), *Doctor Zhivago* (1965), and *A Passage to India* (1984)—and a further six nominations, including Moustapha Akkad's *The Message* (1976), Peter Weir's *Witness* (1985), Michael Apted's *Gorillas in the* Mist (1988), and Jerry Zucker's *Ghost* (1990).

For the scene in which *Lawrence of Arabia's* young servant waits for his master's return, and then sees what appears to be a dot on the shimmering horizon that slowly materializes into Lawrence, David Lean, the producer, asked Jarre to compose "something that tells us what the boy is feeling." As the form of Lawrence comes into view, Jarre's music grows into a sumptuous, heart-stopping crescendo.

For *A Passage to India*, he incorporated Indian motifs to telling effect in a scene where the prudish young Adela Quested (Judy Davis) wanders into a garden of erotic Indian statuary. The music tells us that, beneath the prim exterior, something alarmingly delightful is stirring inside her. Her delicious reverie is shattered by a troupe of monkeys that descend from a nearby tree. Lean had planned on hundreds of monkeys for this scene, but could only obtain five, so he told Jarre: "You have to give me the missing monkeys with your music."

Jarre wrote mainly for orchestras, but in the 1980s, he started to use electronic instruments, notably synthesizers. In *Witness*, for example, he employed a group of 10 synthesists, each one working on sections of the score at the same time, while Jarre conducted them as if for a chamber ensemble. In *Mad Max Beyond Thunderdome* (1985), he augmented the basic symphony orchestra with four grand pianos plus a pipe organ, didgeridoo, fujana, a battery of exotic percussion, and three ondes Martenots. In addition to the sound track for *Witness*, he composed music to striking and sometimes eerie effect in films such as *The Year of Living Dangerously* (1982), *Fatal Attraction* (1987), and *No Way Out* (1987), Luchino Visconti's *The Damned* (1969), John Huston's *The Man Who Would Be King* (1975), Volker Schlöndorff's *The Tin Drum* (1979) and *Circle of Deceit* (1981), and Peter Weir's *Dead Poets Society* (1989).

Jarre added an ingredient that was immeasurable and irreplaceable—music. In conventional research, we tend to measure and analyze the words, and we usually forget the importance of the music. As Maurice Jarre showed us, reaching below the conscious mind with music is what enriches the experience and makes it complete. And so it is when creating a dream: the development of a dream, so essential to inspiring organizations and their leaders to greatness, cannot be based on a subjective whim, a committee consensus, or even conventional research—we are looking for the music. We cannot simply measure the data; we must reach deeper to where the real truth rests below the conscious mind, the same place the music reaches us, which is different from the words.

Many people have subjective views about what a corporate dream should look like, and it is dangerous to make such momentous decisions based on "hunch," prejudice, bias, or majority vote—or even conventional research methodologies. Many leadership decisions—across sectors and issues—are made largely through intuition, or "gut instinct." They are, in the end, intelligently derived "best guesses." Leaders then often use tools, such as traditional market research, commissioned studies, and the opinions of those around them, to validate their best subjective guesses, even though these methods, as described earlier, have routinely been shown to be flawed. Sometimes this "research" is used to justify or "validate" personal biases or subjective opinions.

Permission Space:
The Foundation for the ONE Dream

One cannot build a dream without a foundation. We call the foundation "Permission Space" defined as, "all of the energy freely available and offered to an organization from its relevant constituents—where inspiration lies and is available to be harnessed." Constituents are all those who can affect the future of an entity—and who can therefore accelerate the realization of the ONE Dream. And one cannot build a dream without permission space.

For over 100 years, many Americans, and many citizens of other nations, too, had dreamed about the day a black president would be elected in the United States. Some people of color had even made a run for the office. While such a dream was cherished by many, for all those years it lacked the necessary *permission space* for that dream to be realized—until 2008, when, finally, a surge of sufficient permission space created the outpouring of passion that *inspired* the election of Barack Obama.

The permission space necessary to support the ONE Dream is revealed through a unique research methodology called Scientific Intelligence™.[13] Its use leads to a sound and rigorously determined assessment of the inspired energy available for any given project, brand launch, strategy, or plan for change. Based on recent

---

[13] For a more detailed explanation of Scientific Intelligence™, see www.secretan.com/scientificintelligence

advances in the behavioral sciences, holography, and logic/mathematics, the formula of Scientific Intelligence for enabling organizations to identify the permission space is designed to reveal or establish

- a clear picture of the available energy that all relevant constituents (all those whose relationship with the organization can affect its future) are willing to freely contribute, and which can therefore be harnessed to power the ONE Dream (think of the passion and energy of committed iPhone customers or wiki contributors);
- where inspiration resides;
- a deep and clear understanding of marketplace needs and the source of future sustainability;
- comprehensive yet focused insights about current social attitudes, yearnings, and aspirations;
- the opportunity to bring order and discipline to corporate messaging;
- an accelerated sense of focus—ONEness—across the entire organization and among constituents;
- insights that will lead to the successful and sustainable implementation of the ONE Dream;
- a custodial group that will begin a system-wide review of the implications of the ONE Dream.

This proprietary new research methodology identifies the permission space, which is quite literally the core "DNA" of the ONE Dream—its music—and therefore provides the key drivers of success that will inspire the organization to advance towards that ONE Dream.

The most distinct advantage of the Scientific Intelligence process is its ability to bypass the unconscious filters that often lead respondents to give the false or skewed answers we described earlier. This methodology works on the principle that the public mind has a very specific but largely invisible "belief structure" composed of paths and key "stations" much like the neural structure of the brain. This belief structure accounts for why certain ideas, brands, and products experience unexpected success, whereas others fail to capture the public's imagination, or why some organizations are inspiring and others are not. Understanding and utilizing that belief structure is the only consistent and reliable way to understand public opinion and measure the energy available to support a strategy. Using this methodology ensures that the ONE Dream truly reflects both the passion of the organization and the permission space that the organization has available to realize it. The result inspires, because it is flowing positively with the unconscious energy of a market, team, or group, rather than using negative energy to try to control, alter, or manipulate their behavior—inspiration instead of motivation.[14]

Identifying, Realizing, and Sustaining the ONE Dream

As mentioned earlier, there are three phases to the ONE Dream process:

1. *Identifying* the ONE Dream
2. *Realizing* the ONE Dream
3. *Sustaining* the ONE Dream

I estimate that 10 percent of the energy and time is required to successfully complete Phase 1, 20 percent to complete Phase 2, and 70 percent to complete Phase 3. After the initial euphoria of charting an inspiring new direction, and following the excitement of execution and implementation, sustaining a dream is by far the greatest challenge.

---

[14] A discussion about the difference between "Motivation" and "Inspiration" can be found in Reflection Twelve.

Harriet Tubman said, "Every great dream begins with a dreamer. Always remember, you have within you the strength, the patience, and the passion to reach for the stars to change the world." How do inspiring leaders help to identify and realize a dream? Think about the circus or the state fair—remember those "plate spinners" at the circus, performers who spin plates on the ends of sticks? Typically, after they get about seven or eight of them going, the first one starts to wobble, and they then have to race back to that first plate and re-spin it, thus maintaining its momentum. This process is repeated with all of the plates to keep them from falling. Inspiring leaders are plate spinners—their role is to keep the plates spinning, and the plates represent the inspiration of others. Dropping a plate happens when we do anything that is uninspiring or demoralizing because it sucks the passion from the dream by dampening the permission space. The role for the leader is to never do anything that is uninspiring or demotivating to any of those people—clients, employees, or associates, regulators, unions, vendors, and communities—who, without any dropped plates, are inspired and therefore united in their efforts to achieve the dream. Thus leaders are directly responsible for inspiring and coaching those who are realizing the dream, and who must be fully inspired to live their lives in a way that inspires others—no dropped plates. The purpose of this team of leaders, therefore, is to be inspiring and to ensure that they are inspiring everyone, every day, all the time, in every way, in every communication and action, so that every decision, conversation, feeling, and relationship moves customers and colleagues closer to the realization of their ONE Dream. The first act that demoralizes someone who is trying to realize a dream will break the spell, trash the passion, and waste the opportunity.[15]

Once we have identified the ONE Dream, the passion for realizing and sustaining it comes from integrating what we have cov-

---

[15] I invite you to take the Inspire Pledge at www.secretan.com/inspirepledge

ered so far in this book: understanding why we are here—living our Destiny, Character, and Calling (following our North Star), honoring the sacredness in each other, building relationships that engage each other's energy, and what we shall cover next—living to a set of values that inspire and are inspiring. We don't need charts and graphs and matrices and complex theories for this. It's pretty simple. When we think about what's possible, even if never attained before, and identify it as a dream that we hold dear and seek to realize, and then make the commitment to align the entire team that is serving the customer—and the customer themselves—behind everything necessary to achieve that dream, then the dream becomes possible. As Christopher Reeve said, "So many of our dreams at first seem impossible, then they seem improbable, and then, they seem inevitable." Identifying the ONE Dream that gathers and galvanizes the passion of all constituents is a vital step in igniting the spark of inspiration.

Martin Luther King, Jr. showed us how—so did John F. Kennedy. So can you.

If you want to build a ship, don't drum up people together to collect wood and don't assign them tasks and work, but rather teach them to long for the endless immensity of the sea.

Antoine de Saint-Exupéry

PART TWO

THE FLAME
How Will You Inspire and Lead?

The spark ignites the flame—the fire within us, our passion and intensity, our informed and generous guidance with which we light the way for others. Our flame illuminates and provides warmth. It is bright, always available, and nourishing. It is how others experience us and are therefore inspired by us. The flame is powered by the way we live, and particularly by how we live out our values, because it is through their experience of us that others are served and grow, and the world becomes a better place. People learn and develop, and we affect positive change in the world, because of *who* we are, more than because of what we know. The values we live by are remembered by everyone we touch because they are what inspires them. This is how we begin to create a personal legacy.

Once you have defined the raison d'être of your life—your Destiny, Character, and Calling; your Why-Be-Do—described it in brief words that inspire you and others, and grown into living it daily, learned to build stronger relationships, and identified your ONE Dream, you have achieved the significant and necessary steps in the process of being an inspired and inspiring being, and leader.

The next step is to introduce a set of values that you will live by, and that will enable you to grow and flourish. They are the principles that guide us as we make a difference in the world; they are what other people experience when we touch their lives and inspire them to greater things. We call these the *CASTLE Principles*. I have written extensively about these Principles in other books,[16] so I will not go over already-plowed ground here—except to say that hundreds of thousands of people who have attended our Higher Ground Leadership retreats, workshops, and seminars are living inspired lives today through their practice. Many organizations have adopted them as their corporate values, too. I hope you will find them equally valuable.

CASTLE is an acronym that stands for Courage, Authenticity, Service, Truthfulness, Love, and Effectiveness. When fully lived, these principles are the path to becoming free from living small, uninspiring lives, enabling us instead to live bright lives as a flame that lights the way for others, making a difference and lifting their spirits.[17]

In the six Reflections that follow, we will illuminate each of these values individually and consider how the CASTLE Principles can change who we are and how we conduct ourselves as Higher Ground Leaders, thus helping us to become more inspired and lead lives that also inspire others to make a difference in the world.

---

[16] ONE: *The Art and Practice of Conscious Leadership*; The Secretan Center Inc., 2006, and *Inspire! What Great Leaders Do*; John Wiley and Sons, 2004
[17] Use the CASTLE Organizational Survey as a cultural barometer in your own organization to measure the degree to which your employees feel the organization is practicing the CASTLE Principles, and to assess the entire organization's cultural health. See www.secretan.com/castleorgsurvey.
To assess your own personal CASTLE score, visit www.secretan.com/castlepersonalsurvey.

Reflection Six: COURAGE

Argue for your limitations, and sure enough, they are yours.

Richard Bach

Merriam-Webster's Dictionary defines courage as "mental or moral strength to venture, persevere, and withstand danger, fear, or difficulty." Inspiring leaders embody mental, moral, and spiritual courage because followers abhor cowards and love leaders with mettle—it's as simple as that. And smart leaders do what works.

One of the ways in which we use the word courage is in reference to the bold actions of firefighters, police officers, and paramedics at their best, or to those of whistle-blowers who expose corporate corruption. In the first instance, a person's life is in danger due to the physical risks being taken; in the second case, people are risking their jobs by telling the truth—one is physically courageous and the other is morally courageous.

In corporate life, we are only infrequently required to display physical courage; but we are required to display moral courage almost daily. We cannot follow our North Star—our Why-Be-Do—without courage, nor our ONE Dream. All these require courage. Not enough leaders rise to this call, and those who do are inspiring.

Conventional wisdom tells us that breakthroughs in life cannot be made without enormous effort sustained over a long period of time. In every field, there are many entrenched, traditional beliefs that present insurmountable hurdles to achieving the remarkable. This thinking is old-fashioned and unnecessary.

Courage, Breakthroughs, and Skiing

Consider the art of skiing, for instance. For some, this sport is dangerous and frightening. When I am guiding and teaching people on the mountain (see the Leadership Summit described in Reflection Three), I regularly enable skiers of intermediate ability—usually leaders—to overcome their fears so that they can ski moguls (bumps) in their first half day and double-black diamond runs ("experts only" terrain) by the end of the first day. Many teachers will say this is impossible—but we do it all the time. We do this because it is a metaphor—as it goes on the mountain, so it goes at work. The United States ski industry, for example, includes 600 resorts, 29,000 professional ski instructors, and 26,000 ski patrollers, and although many excellent instructors (and, as mentioned earlier, I am an accredited ski instructor myself) help skiers and boarders to advance their skills, many lack the ability or will to do so, and thus those they teach rarely advance their skills in a meaningful way. Consequently, it is unusual to find rapid, radical breakthroughs in skiing or boarding ability, especially among skiers who have skied for a long time and whose skills have plateaued.

The "business" of leadership has the same structure, with many excellent teachers making meaningful change and helping leaders to grow, and many others stuck in an unimaginative rut—consultants, academics, writers for learned journals, training executives, and coaches—still teaching old ideas in new times. As in skiing, leaders who have practiced their craft for many years, and whose skills have plateaued, find change and radical reinvention the most difficult. As an expert teacher of leadership and inspiration, I am part of a team that helps organizations and individuals achieve similarly radical breakthroughs in inspiring leadership in a remarkably short period of time, as we do in skiing. The secret to making a breakthrough in leadership or skiing is the same—courage and trust.

Breaking through Limitations

It amazes me that so many skiers remain average or mediocre year after year, when they could do much better. And I am equally amazed to see the same thing happen again and again in organizations. All this suggests that we are losing the strength of our courage muscles, because more than anything else, change requires courage.

In choosing how we lead, we exercise similar self-imposed limitations. Yet people regularly achieve breakthroughs in their experiences, in the meaning and fulfillment of their work, in the results they are able to inspire from people they lead, in the fortunes they are able to make from doing what they love—and all of us have the power to do the same. As Buckminster Fuller said, we must "dare to be naïve," and naïveté can best be achieved through "unlearning"—but unlearning requires courage.[18]

We are able to teach leaders how to ski better and how to lead better in a fraction of the time that most people expect by igniting passion, willingness to learn and change, and a desire to improve—and most importantly, a firm belief that there are no limits. When we do this, we are the flame that burns brightly for others, inspiring and encouraging them, and coaching and guiding them to Higher Ground. We call this courage.

The Leader as Courage Coach, Mentor, and Guide

Recently, I took a group of leaders to the top of a 12,400-foot mountain. They were visiting with me in my mountain home to

---

[18] See "Unlearning Is a Precondition for Effectiveness" in Reflection Eleven.

learn how to make breakthroughs in their skiing and leadership skills.

As we disembarked from the surface lift at the top, a sudden snowstorm appeared, carrying big winds and causing visibility to decline to about eight feet. We were the only people at the top of the mountain, with no way down except on our skis. I huddled with my team in the storm.

"Here is the plan," I told them. "The only way off this peak is to ski down the side of the mountain into the valley below, for about 1,000 feet, as quickly as we can, in order to build up enough speed that will help us to accelerate as we shoot up the other side. The route doesn't have many bumps or ruts, but it is quite steep. We won't be able to see anything, and you don't know the mountain. So, I will ski first, because I know the terrain like the back of my hand." Laura McCafferty volunteered to follow first. "If you agree, I would like you to ski right behind me as close as possible," I told her, "then everyone else can follow one after the other. Watch my skis—it will be the only thing you will be able to see in the whiteout. If you see the tails of my skis going up and down, you will know I've just gone over a bump and you can brace yourself accordingly. If my skis turn, follow the direction they take. Trust me—we are going to be OK."

It went exactly as planned: a team of courageous, trusting, and safe skiers and leaders high-fived their success after we zoomed into the gloom together and arrived safely on the other side—all in one piece.

When we dare, it causes a moment of insecurity, but when we hold back, or try to play it safe, it causes us to waste our potential. We should aspire to live the other side of safety—and this side of danger. T.S. Eliot said, "Only those who will risk going too far can possibly find out how far one can go." Remember, your current safe boundaries were once unknown frontiers.

Courage and Trust

Six months later, this ski group held a reunion telephone call and we relived our experience and the euphoria it had generated at the time. "What is this 'trust' and 'courage' that makes for the essential components of leadership?" I asked. "We know how important it is, but how is it acquired or bestowed? Every leader wants to know this." One person replied, "I trusted you because you loved me—I could see it in your eyes and I knew you wouldn't ask me to do something that was dangerous." This got me thinking about how important love is in building trust. Another said, "On the first day, you explained how to ski moguls, then you demonstrated it, then you asked us to do it, then you explained and coached us. I trusted you from then on because you helped us to grow without endangering us." *The other side of safety—this side of danger.* Another said, "You never forced us to go beyond our potential competence—out of our comfort zone, yes, but not beyond our potential mastery." And another said, "You didn't buy into my fear—you simply didn't think that my fears were justified. I thought about your view of me and decided that I liked it better than the view I had of myself—so I decided to trust you."

We had fun, we grew and learned together, we skied in magnificent surroundings, we laughed a lot, we stretched ourselves, and we looked out for each other.

It is clear, then, that in teaching and leading others, there are some essential elements. The leader/teacher[19] (and we are always both) must earn and build a trusting relationship with the follower. This trust creates a *loving*[20] space in which experimentation and challenge can occur, and in which we are able to let go of certainties. This leads to change—and in change there is

---

[19] In the dictionary definition, a leader is one who *shows how to*, and a teacher is one who *shows the way to*.
[20] See Reflection Ten for a deeper discussion about the CASTLE Principle "Love."

power. It takes little courage to cling to the stillness of the status quo—it is movement and change, which involve letting go of the familiar while embracing the new, that require courage. Paradoxically, safety comes from the adventurous and the exciting, not the failing systems of the past. In this way, we sacrifice what we are for what we can become—and that takes courage.

As Maya Angelou has put it, "One isn't necessarily born with courage, but one is born with potential. Without courage, we cannot practice any other virtue with consistency. We can't be kind, true, merciful, generous, or honest."

It takes courage to do those things that people so admire in great leaders: being vulnerable, admitting a mistake, apologizing, telling others that we love them, listening, empathizing, abandoning a flawed decision, changing habits that no longer serve us, standing for integrity, and risking failure or criticism—these all require courage—and doing any of them inspires others.

Courage, trust, and love are magic and essential ingredients for leaders in quest of the extraordinary.

The surprising thing about the CASTLE Principles is that they are within us already. There is nothing new for any of us to learn—we already own the capacity. We become inspiring when we recall any of the CASTLE Principles that we have underutilized, bring them strongly into our awareness, practice them, and live them every day—starting with Courage.

All men should strive to learn before they die,
what they are running from, and to, and why.

James Thurber

Reflection Seven: AUTHENTICITY

If you call forth what is in you, it will save you.
If you do not call forth what is in you, it will
destroy you.

The Gospel of Saint Thomas

When we are authentic, we are living from our essential self; whenever we deny a truth, we are living from the social self—in other words, inauthentically. As Freya Madeline Starke phrased it, "There can be no happiness if the things we believe in are different from the things we do."

And there we have the essence of authenticity—it is the capacity to be in alignment with the essential self.

How many people do you know who say one thing, but do another? Or who think one thing and then say another? Or who feel one thing, but do another? Or who say but do different things all the time, causing you to think of them as unreliable or inconsistent?

Authenticity is the alignment of head, mouth, heart, and feet—thinking, saying, feeling, and doing the same thing—consistently. This builds trust, and followers *love* leaders they can trust.

One of the most obvious examples of inauthenticity is the inability to admit mistakes—to own personal fallibility. Here is where the ego has a very loud voice—not the usual incessant and misleading whispering—but a yelling in our ear of the spurious message that if we accept responsibility for making a mistake, it will make us look incompetent, flawed, and lead to personal loss or hardship, or even reprisals and punishments.

Corporate Authenticity

Look closely into any industry and you will find layers of authenticity and inauthenticity. The health-care industry provides just one startling example. Studies show that in the United States one of every 100 hospital patients suffers negligent treatment, 100,000 people die each year from prescription drugs, while over-the-counter medications kill another 40,000, and medical errors are responsible for another 195,000 deaths. As alarming as these figures are—nearly 350,000 preventable deaths in health care each year—this may be an underestimate: studies also show that as few as 30 percent of medical errors are revealed to patients. And a Rand Corporation study estimated that one-third or more of the $2.2 trillion spent on health-care treatments in America—$7,500 per person—could be of little value.

In health care, risk managers, malpractice lawyers, and insurers generally counsel health professionals, doctors, and hospitals to "deny and defend," warning clients that any admission of a mistake, or even an expression of regret, could lead to media and reputational fallout, loss of business, litigation, and endangered—even ruined—careers. So the general practice has been to deny liability or fault—an example of unrepentant inauthenticity—and this in an industry whose ruling precept is the Hippocratic oath: *Primum non nocere* (First do no harm). And according to Dr. Lucian L. Leape, an authority on patient safety at Harvard, most doctors feel the same way. "We're pushing uphill on this. Most doctors don't really believe that if they're open and honest with patients, they won't be sued," he says.

Dr. Tapas K. Das Gupta is the chairman of surgical oncology at the University of Illinois Medical Center at Chicago, and a highly regarded cancer surgeon. After viewing the X-ray that showed that he had opened up a patient and removed the wrong sliver of tissue, in this case a segment of the eighth rib instead of the ninth, he did an unusual thing: he acknowledged his error directly to the patient, and told her he was deeply sorry. Having never made such a serious error in 40 years of practice, he told his patient and her husband, "After all these years, I cannot give you any excuse whatsoever. It is just one of those things that occurred. I have to some extent harmed you."

Though most health-care lawyers would wince at such an admission, the dramatic rise in malpractice costs and demands for action against medical errors have caused a handful of leading academic medical centers, including those at Harvard, Johns Hopkins, and Stanford universities, and the University of Michigan, to try a more authentic approach. The Veterans Health Administration, which pioneered the practice of open disclosure at its hospital in Lexington, Kentucky, in the late 1980s, now requires all adverse events, even those that are not obvious, to be disclosed.

Malpractice lawyers agree that what makes patients mad is not so much the errors as their concealment—the blatant deception and the injured party's concern that it might happen again. By quickly disclosing medical errors and offering genuine apologies, along with fair compensation, some health-care leaders are attempting to reverse the loss of integrity perceived by the public, realizing that to do so will enable them to divert precious resources from costly and protracted lawsuits and channel them into learning from mistakes, while simultaneously diminishing the anger and frustration that so often feed a lawsuit.

Of course, the social selves of many attorneys will leap into the foreground upon hearing this news, prompting dark warnings that disclosure will result in a flood of lawsuits—but the opposite is true. Many hospitals are reporting decreases in their caseloads and savings in legal costs, and in some cases, malpractice premiums have declined.

At the University of Michigan Health System, one of the early leaders in authentic full disclosure, existing claims and lawsuits between August 2001 and August 2007 dropped from 262 to 83, according to Richard C. Boothman, the medical center's chief risk officer.

"Improving patient safety and patient communication is more likely to cure the malpractice crisis than defensiveness and denial," Mr. Boothman said, adding, "The hospital's legal defense costs and the money it must set aside to pay claims have each been cut by two-thirds." The time taken to dispose of cases has been halved at the University of Michigan Health System.

This change in philosophy has engendered a new mood and relationship between trial lawyers and Mr. Boothman: the lawyers know that Mr. Boothman will offer prompt and fair compensation for real negligence, but will stand firm in defending doctors when the hospital believes that appropriate care has been provided.

According to Southfield, Michigan, trial lawyer Norman D. Tucker, "The filing of a lawsuit at the University of Michigan is now the last option, whereas with other hospitals it tends to be the first and only option. We might give cases a second look before filing because if it's not going to settle quickly, tighten up your cinch. It's probably going to be a long ride."

At the University of Illinois, greater authenticity has produced the same results: the number of malpractice filings dropped by 50 percent in the first two years since the adoption of its program of authentic disclosure, according to Dr. Timothy B. McDonald, the hospital's chief safety and risk officer.

In one case, the hospital discovered an electrode that had dislodged from a baby's scalp during a Caesarian section. The mother, Maria Del Rosario Valdez, said that although she was unhappy about having a second operation to retrieve the wire, she appreciated that it was an accidental error. Her sister urged her to retain a lawyer, but she chose not to do so because she wished to avoid the angst of a lawsuit and believed that her injuries were not severe enough to justify pursuing a legal remedy.

Ms. Valdez said she was satisfied that the hospital quickly acknowledged its mistake, corrected it without charge, and introduced procedures for keeping better track of electrodes in the future. "They took the time to explain it and to tell me they were sorry," she said. "I felt good that they were taking care of what they had done."

We love authenticity and despise duplicity and flimflam. Out of the 37 cases where the University of Illinois Medical Center acknowledged a preventable error and apologized, only one patient filed suit and only six settlements exceeded the medical and related expenses associated with the cases.

In Dr. Das Gupta's case in 2006, the patient, a young nurse, retained a lawyer, but in the end chose not to sue, settling for a payment of $74,000 from the hospital. Said her lawyer, David J. Pritchard, "She told me that the doctor was completely candid, completely honest, and so frank that she and her husband—usually the husband wants to pound the guy—that all the anger was gone. His apology helped get the case settled for a lower amount of money." The patient received about $40,000 after paying medical and legal expenses and had the surgery done at another hospital, where she learned that there was no cancer present. "You have no idea what a relief that was," Dr. Das Gupta said.

Straightforward, isn't it? The authenticity of a simple apology—the ego permitting—can cut costs, reduce anger, shorten legal proceedings, create learning opportunities, and bring the opposing parties to a place of conciliation. Transparency, openness, and authenticity are necessary conditions for getting to this place. Given the obvious evidence of these and so many other examples, it is a wonder that all leaders do not yet appreciate what inspiring leaders have learned: authenticity raises performance standards.

Personal Authenticity

Corporate authenticity is simply the sum of the personal authenticity of those in the corporation. Oddly, we find it easier to be authentic with others than we do with ourselves. And we find it easier to discuss the authenticity—or lack of it—of others or other organizations, than we do to *be* authentic ourselves.

And just as we find inauthentic organizations distasteful, we find inauthentic individuals equally so. And the reverse is true—we are inspired by authentic organizations, mainly because their cultures encourage and nourish authentic behavior, attracting employees and customers who value authenticity.

Whistle-blowers are examples of extreme authenticity, and while most of us will not be called upon to demonstrate such extraordinary levels of authenticity, the role of the whistle-blower represents a powerful benchmark for individual genuineness and courage. If we are to be inspiring leaders, then reciprocal authenticity is demanded first in our relationships with those inside our organizations and teams, and secondly, with those outside the organization. Note the order here—we cannot expect to inspire customers, suppliers, regulators, and unions with our authenticity if we cannot even practice this principle with those on our home team.

Authenticity: A Lesson We All Get—Eventually

Our ego—our social self—wraps itself in the cloak of inauthenticity. But every one of us will eventually shed this veneer, even if, for some of us, it is not until our final moments on this mortal plane. Everyone eventually gets it—some sooner than others—but no one leaves without this lesson.

Eugene Desmond O'Kelly worked for three decades for the giant accounting firm KPMG International, ultimately claiming the position of chairman and chief executive. A graduate of Pennsylvania State University, with an MBA from Stanford University, Gene O'Kelly joined KPMG in San Francisco in 1972, became a partner in 1982, and was appointed to the management committee in 1998.

As he neared his fifty-third birthday, he was the epitome of the hard-charging American executive—guiding the direction of 20,000 employees, focusing on changing the culture, managing corporate strategy, paying $465 million to settle charges of criminal tax fraud, racking up endless frequent flyer miles, entertaining clients—and sacrificing home and family life. He was feeling, as he would later say, "vigorous, indefatigable, and damn near immortal."

The ground shifted beneath him in the spring of 2005, when he received the news that he had inoperable late-stage brain cancer. This news was accompanied by the realization that he would probably not make it through the summer. Suddenly, the wisdom kicked in: in his typical A-type behavior, he catalogued his colleagues, friends, and family into five concentric circles, with the inner circle representing those closest to him, and he realized that he had been, "a bit too consumed by the outermost circle. Perhaps I could have found the time, in the last decade, to have had a weekday lunch with my wife more often than...twice? I realized that being able to count a thousand people in that fifth circle was not something to be proud of. It was something to be wary of."

In the 100 days between diagnosis and his passing in September of 2005, Gene O'Kelly wrote a book (*Chasing Daylight: How My Forthcoming Death Transformed My Life*; McGraw-Hill, 2007) in which he would allow that one should confront one's own mortality sooner rather than later. But the paradox of being so organized in his death was not lost on him. "While I do believe that the business mindset is, in important ways, useful at the end of life, it sounds pretty weird to try to be CEO of one's own death... Given the profoundness of dying, and how different its quality felt from the life I led, I had to undo at least as many business habits as I tried to maintain." And so he began to meditate in the mornings, to search for great moments, to transition into the next state, and reflect on his legacy for his two daughters. He met with his colleagues, friends, and family, to "close" their relationships. And he came to realize that his thinking had been too narrow and his boundaries too strict.

"Had I known then what I know now," he said, "almost certainly I would have been more creative in figuring out a way to live a more balanced life, to spend more time with my family." His widow, Corinne, says this was his one regret. Although he had begun to find a better balance before he became sick, he ran out of time.

Authenticity is about being real, transparent, and balanced. Authentic people are more committed to *being* than doing (the *Be* of the *Why-Be-Do*)—to living openly in ways that inspire others. And most importantly, when we are authentic, we are honoring the essential self.

The Importance of Authenticity for Corporate Governance

In her book *The Seven Signs of Ethical Collapse: How to Spot Moral Meltdowns in Companies...Before It's Too Late*, (St. Martin's Press, 2006), Marianne Jennings, professor of legal and ethical studies at the W. P. Carey School of Business, has defined the seven warning signs of companies ruled by out-of-control egos—the social self on steroids, inauthenticity exemplified—that have led to the ethical collapse of such train wrecks as HealthSouth, WorldCom, Lehman Brothers, Washington Mutual, Adelphia, and Enron. These include:

1. *Pressure to meet those numbers*—unreasonable and unrealistic obsession with meeting quantitative goals; companies in the grip of numbers-pressure stray from authenticity in their pursuit of impossible goals;
2. *Fear and silence*—moral meltdown fed by fear, silence, and sycophancy; sustaining an inauthentic myth requires the silencing of protestors;
3. *Young 'uns and a bigger-than-life CEO*—the presence of an iconic CEO who is adored by the community, the

media, and just about anyone at a distance; who is surrounded by a sycophantic management team, often made up of young, inexperienced direct-reports who are "hooked on the cash and the trappings" of executive life—and therefore have no authentic dialogue with the leader;

4. *Weak board*—the boards of companies at risk of ethical collapse are weak and ineffectual; often these boards are populated by friends of the management team; some are compromised by conflict; others are cowed by the icon; all engage in inauthentic dialogue. Replacing the board with a stronger group requires a vigorous return to true authenticity;

5. *A culture of conflicts (as in conflicts of interest)*—the people running these companies come to think that the business exists for the benefit of themselves and their cronies, and authentic feedback from employees, board members, customers, and suppliers is ignored or suppressed;

6. *Innovation like no other (or, companies who believe they are completely different from all other companies)*—Jennings writes: "These companies and those in charge see themselves as visionaries who could reinvent business." Hubris is the shadow of authenticity;

7. *Goodness in some areas atones for evil in others*—nearly all ethically bankrupt companies shroud themselves in the inauthenticity of faux philanthropy and social goodness, hoping this will offset cooked books, fraud, or insider trading—all the usual activities of ethical collapse.

As professor Jennings advises us, fostering a corporate culture of authenticity will encourage employees to let their true voices be heard—to be authentic themselves. The curricula of many business schools have for years taught MBA students to practice behavior that falls within ethically approved parameters—and, of course, the law—while failing to teach integrity, transparency, and authenticity. This has led to the creation of double standards that encouraged executives to accept fraud as long as the company was being "socially responsible."

If we recalibrate our standards of personal authenticity, we will restore corporate trust—the touchstone of the inspiring leader—so earnestly needed in the modern corporation. Of course, it is an enduring paradox that in an authentic organization, performance increases because the leaders take the strong medicine needed to *authentically* turn things around, while ethically bankrupt leaders engage in inauthentic, devious acts to conceal disappointing performance, which leads to a steeper decline.

We lead because of who we are—our authentic, essential selves—more than from what we do. We become inspired—and therefore inspiring to others—when we live from the principles we value most, rather than by the external forces of the social self.

In the words of Snoop Dog, "You got to be who you are when you are."

So you see, this CASTLE Principle of Authenticity is already within you, too. There is nothing new for you to learn, just the need to raise awareness of it, and practice it, and live it daily. Authentic people inspire others.

Follow the grain in your own wood.

Howard Thurman

Reflection Eight: SERVICE

If I can stop one heart from breaking,
I shall not live in vain.
If I can ease one life the aching,
Or cool one pain,
Or help one fainting robin
Unto his nest again,
I shall not live in vain.

Emily Dickinson

When faced with life's threatening situations, we often respond with default behavior—fear or attack—and typically, this is based on serving the social self. Even those of us who might hold Jesus Christ, Buddha, Mother Teresa, or Martin Luther King, Jr. as our personal heroes, can still fail to recognize that when we stray into self-serving, fear-based, or attacking responses, we are neither Christ-like nor effective. At the intellectual level, we understand that the response of a Buddha or Christ, for example, would always be authentic love, compassion, and service—under any circumstances. Even though we know this to be true, the judgmental tune detectable in this message can sometimes grate and make it sound like pretentious sermonizing that is naïvely disconnected from the reality of our day-to-day lives. After all, we reason, if we were attacked by a mugger, the natural reaction would be based on safeguarding our own needs resulting in fear or attack—or both. But not for everybody.

Not, for example, for Julio Diaz, a 31-year-old social worker from New York, who had practiced the same evening routine for years—a one-hour trip home on the subway, exiting one stop early, which took him to his favorite diner for his end-of-day meal.

On February, 2008, Diaz disembarked from the No. 6 train onto a nearly deserted platform and headed for the stairs towards the exit. Suddenly, he found his way barred by a knife-wielding teenage boy.

Said Diaz, "He wants my money, so I just gave him my wallet and told him, 'Here you go.'"

As the teen sought to merge into the shadows, Diaz called out to him, "Hey, wait a minute. You forgot something. If you're going to be robbing people for the rest of the night, you might as well take my coat to keep you warm."

The look on the mugger's face registered, "Like, what's going on here?" said Diaz later. "He asked me, 'Why are you doing this?'"

Diaz looked squarely at his young assailant: "If you're willing to risk your freedom for a few dollars, then I guess you must really need the money. I mean, all I wanted to do was get dinner, and if you really want to join me...hey, you're more than welcome."

Diaz instinctively chose authentic compassion rather than aggression or fear: "You know I just felt maybe he really needs help."

The two went to Diaz' favorite diner together and settled into two seats in a booth. Soon, Diaz recounted, "The manager comes by, the dishwashers come by, the waiters come by to say hi and the kid was like, 'You know everybody here. Do you own this place?'"

"No, I just eat here a lot," replied Diaz.

The boy's eyes widened in amazement: "But you're even nice to the dishwasher."

Diaz asked, "Well, haven't you been taught you should be nice to everybody?"

"Yea, but I didn't think people actually behaved that way," the teen replied, still not sure if he was witnessing reality.

When he asked the boy what he wanted out of life, Diaz said, "He just had almost a sad face." The teen didn't seem to have an answer.

When the server presented the bill, Diaz was faced with a dilemma—how was he going to pay? Diaz passed the problem to the teen, "Look, I guess you're going to have to pay for this bill 'cause you have my money and I can't pay for this. So if you give me my wallet back, I'll gladly treat you."

The boy "didn't even think about it," returning the wallet almost instinctively, Diaz said. "I gave him $20...I figure maybe it'll help him. I don't know."

Then Diaz used a cunning ploy; he asked the boy for something in return—his knife—"...and he gave it to me."

Diaz' mother later said, "You're the type of kid that if someone asked you for the time, you gave them your watch."

"I figure, you know, if you treat people right, you can only hope that they treat you right. It's as simple as it gets in this complicated world."

It's as simple as it gets in this complicated world.

Simple wisdom, too: Serving others is a sure way to inspire them—and that's as simple as it gets in this complicated world.

People First

Of course, the question is, "Serve whom?" The answer? "Everyone," because we are all inspired the same way. But there is a preferred ranking of "everyone."

And this brings us to the perplexing issue of why so many leaders fail to understand that at the top of the list of people we need to inspire through service are those with whom we work—employees, associates, colleagues, and team members. If there is any priority ranking at all, then employees should top the list, followed by customers, then shareholders and suppliers.

A story is told about Southwest Airlines, which received a letter from a woman complaining about the absence of seat assignments, a first-class section, and meals. She also didn't like the boarding procedure, or the flight attendants' sporty uniforms, or the casual atmosphere. To top it off, she abhorred peanuts! Southwest answers every customer letter, but this one stumped them. So the letter drifted through the hierarchy onto the desk of then-chairman Herb Kelleher for advice and inspiration. In sixty seconds, the legendary Herb had penned this response: "Dear Mrs. Crabapple, We'll miss you. Love, Herb." Southwest Airlines has been consistent in its commitment to its employees for over 43 years. Said Colleen Barrett, Southwest's former president, "Our customer service package is totally dependent upon [our] employees. Without employees—and without the right employees—we would have at best poor customer service, and poor service means no more customers." The corporate aspiration that Southwest attempts to live up to each day is this: "Above all, employees will be provided the same concern, respect, and caring attitude within the organization that they are expected to share externally with every Southwest customer."

And there we have the key, exemplified by Southwest's priorities: employees first, then customers, then shareholders—completely upside down from the legacy airlines—and most other businesses.

The most inspiring organizations in the world know that the routinely mouthed mantra, "The customer is our most important asset" is not sound. It's not that customers are not important assets (although the term "asset" is problematic, too, since we don't own them)—the *employee* is the most important asset. If we serve and inspire employees well, they will serve customers; but if we serve customers and overlook employees, or even if we serve customers better or *more* than employees, we will not retain an inspired team that inspires customers and realizes our ONE Dream.

Yet survey after survey shows that fear and intimidation, power, and aggressive behavior—sometimes passive aggressive behavior—amongst employees and their leaders are the norm in corporate life. My experience testifies to this reality. Much of my work with leaders of major corporations seeks to inspire them to break their ingrained dysfunctional habits that sap passion, creativity, and inspiration, and seeks instead to grow the will to serve—first each other—the first team, as Patrick Lencioni calls it,[21] and then everyone else. We labor under the misunderstanding that it's OK to abuse each other as long as we make the numbers. But as Colleen Barrett reminds us, dysfunctional employees generate a scarcity of customers. What's sad, too, is that *dysfunctional employees generate dysfunctional customers.*

The principle of service—especially to each other—rests on the concept of oneness: the reality that we are all one and interconnected with everything. Failure to serve employees results in a decline in their energy, passion, positive attitude, and willingness to learn and to serve others. Customers sense this, and the level of service they experience declines as a result; this feeds back to employees, sapping their inspiration and deepening the negative cycle—it is all one. And when this happens, flames are extinguished.

Service as Partnership—Not War

The "old story" of leadership makes marketing a warrior practice. Warrior marketers pursue the conquest and domination of markets, crush the competition, develop "killer applications" and strategies, and disrupt markets with "category killers." The war-

---

[21] Lencioni, Patrick, *The Five Dysfunctions of a Team: A Leadership Fable*; Jossey-Bass, 2002

rior mentality, epitomized for many business leaders in Sun Tzu's *The Art of War* and such "gems" as Wess Roberts' *Leadership Secrets of Attila the Hun,* deploys tricks and cunning to extract as much from the customer's pocketbook as the law will permit— think about the indecipherable loan or credit card contract you have with your bank. All this testosterone serves the social self and the ego and the attainment of short-term results. But the "New Story" of leadership seeks to collaborate with employees and customers through symbiosis, feedback, compassionate input, cooperation, and deep listening—and most important of all, empathy, *feeling* what other people *feel*, in order to develop relevant new products and services that inspire—all practices that recognize and rely on interconnectedness. This is mutual service—what Easterners might call *karma*—the awareness that what we give is what we get. The more we practice warrior behavior, the more it will be returned to us, and the more we serve—honoring the sacredness of the other—the more it will be returned to us, too. We can choose to operate from our social selves or our essential selves. Different results occur, depending on the choices we make.

We Can't Apply Old Solutions to New Problems

One of the greatest risks facing organizations today is applying old solutions to new problems. The key issues and metrics of expanding market share, ramping up stock prices, adding shareholder value, being lean and mean, growth and domination, and wrangling cost and quality problems through the systematic application of, for example, Six Sigma, all speak to problems, many of which were solved long ago. In retrospect, some of the solutions applied, though they seemed to have merit then, look so "last century" now. In fact, within the 58 largest companies that have implemented a Six Sigma program, the share price of 91 percent of them has trailed the S&P 500 index, according to an analysis by Charles Holland of the consulting firm QualPro, Inc. While Six Sigma is an excellent methodology for improving quality and extracting costs from many processes, it is most effective when its left-brain emphasis is infused with compassion, inspiration, and empathy. As inspiring leaders know, there is more to inspiring leadership than driving down defects to 3.4 per million. These issues and metrics represent the "old story" of leadership, which is heavily influenced by the mantra of "making the numbers." But as Harvard Business School's Rakesh Khurana has put it, "That meant a disinvestment in the future. It was a dramatic reversal of everything that made capitalism strong and the envy of the rest of the world: the willingness of a CEO to forgo dividends and make an investment that wouldn't be realized until one or two CEOs down the road." We have arrived, he believes, "…at a hinge point of American capitalism." Foresters have an expression: You never plant trees for yourself; you plant them for your grandchildren.

To be clear, I am not dismissing Lean or Six Sigma, but unless we connect such methodologies to the souls of employees, by *serving* them as passionately as we would our customers, they will remain tools of the social self—barren and uninspiring. We have helped many leaders rework their Six Sigma programs so that the fear and opposition from employees were removed by restoring their faith in these initiatives through first honoring the sacredness of people, and second, searching for quality and process improvements that would not punish them personally.

In many ways, our misguided addiction to the external, the social self, at the personal level, as described earlier, is mirrored in our desire to do the same thing at the corporate level. "Making the numbers," and all that this term implies, causes us to be intensely focused on how we will be judged, what the external world—the likes of Wall Street, shareholders, media, the Board Compensation Committee, Sarbanes-Oxley, academics who write case studies, competitors, and other opinion-shapers—will think of us. And often that means what they will think of *me*, the corporate social self.

The shift to a greater awareness of oneness, towards the honoring of the essential self, leads us to serve *others*—the purpose of any organization. Because we are interconnected, organizations cannot survive for long through self-interest.

The ancient Greeks had a word—*hybris* (from which is derived the term "hubris")—to describe actions which, intentionally or not, shamed and humiliated the victim. It was most frequently displayed in the public and private actions of the powerful and rich. Hybris, though not specifically defined, was a legal term and was considered a crime and also the greatest sin of the ancient Greek world.

Corporate history is littered with organizations undone by hubris and narcissism, as we have seen in Professor Jennings' description in Reflection Seven—an exclusive commitment to the ego. Sooner rather than later, the reality of the *needs of the other* demands our attention, and if we fail to *serve* those needs, our organizations will simply become irrelevant and fade away. Revolutions are born from this inattention. Becoming one with the needs of others, instead of being separated from them, is the essence of service.

This accelerating shift from the "old story" to the "New Story" is strikingly demonstrated by our changing choices of corporate icons. *Fortune* magazine named Jack Welch "manager of the century" in 1999, but a decade later, the new benchmarks for inspiring leadership have become Larry Page, Sergey Brin, and Eric Schmidt at Google; Jeff Bezos at Amazon; and Brad Anderson formerly of Best Buy. What we are learning is that people don't come to work in order to increase market share, destroy the competition, be number one or number two in the marketplace, or to increase the return on assets by three points. These may be important priorities for the organization, but they are not what inspires the hearts of employees. Employees yearn to experience meaning and fulfillment, to make the world better—to *serve.* Given a choice, people come to work to engage their essential selves more than their social selves, and are the most inspired when doing so aligns with their own personal North Star. Indeed, if the ONE Dream of the organization is aligned with, and serves, the *Why-Be-Do* of each employee, we are well on our way to creating inspiring organizations.

People come to work in order to be inspired by those leaders who serve *them* first, customers second, and shareholders third. When we serve, we inspire.

Serving the Needs of Gen X and Gen Y

Our long love affair with shareholder capitalism is being replaced with *stakeholder capitalism.* As we witness this transition, the trained eye can notice that, generally speaking, many leaders are still continuing to apply "old-story" leadership and management theories, even as "New-Story" conditions appear. Whereas the baby boomer generation (1946-1964) championed the shareholder, *Gen X* (1965-1978) and *Gen Y* (1979-2002) employees want to integrate their work and personal lives and are champions of the environment, societal and community needs, support of the disadvantaged, meaning and fulfillment at work, and the greater good. And they rank these equally—or even higher—than increasing shareholder wealth.

Here is where the disconnect chafes—old theories and practices are still being applied to new generations of employees. The enormity of this transition is little understood by many leaders. The American Society of Training and Development predicts that 76 million Americans will retire over the next two decades. Only 46 million will be arriving to replace them. Most of those new workers will be Generation Y-ers. According to Jordan Kaplan, an associate managerial science professor at Long Island University, Brooklyn Campus in New York, "Generation Y is much less likely to respond to the traditional command-and-control type of management still popular in much of today's workforce.

They've grown up questioning their parents, and now they're questioning their employers. They don't know how to shut up, which is great, but that's aggravating to the 50-year-old manager who says, 'Do it and do it now.'" And Generation Y has been called the most high-maintenance, yet potentially most high-performing generation ever. And right alongside this momentous cultural shift, another one is developing—50 percent of those under 20 in America today are from an ethnic minority, and serving their needs will require a new playbook.

The inspiring leader is aware of these challenges and has learned how to engage and serve this diversity. Inspiring leaders understand service at a visceral level and live their lives in this way because they know that it inspires others because it *serves* them. And of course, as employees experience this inspiring leadership, they quickly and efficiently signal to each other where the "cool" workplaces are to be found. It is not a coincidence that Google, Southwest Airlines, Amazon, and Starbucks (even though their short-term fortunes may fluctuate) receive 10 times as many applications as they have available job opportunities, while "old-story" organizations constantly struggle to recruit replacements for those fleeing from their uninspiring environments.

Capitalism that Serves

A relevant question to ask at this point is, "Is serving others and the greater good compatible with serving the interests of shareholders, and are there necessary trade-offs?" The answer, of course, is that there is room for both, but that they must be balanced. Says Terry Mollner, who co-founded the mutual fund company Calvert Group in 1982, "…we're in a new era of consciousness now in which priorities don't need to be hierarchical. The whole hierarchy is in the service of the common good, including profit-making." We will discuss this at greater length in Reflection Eleven—Effectiveness.

Many people living in the West, and a growing number in other parts of the world, are staunch supporters of democratic capitalism. The inspiring leader has awakened to the need to sharpen the focus of our definition of capitalism by acknowledging that we mean *caring capitalism*—capitalism that embraces the interests of everyone, capitalism that will leave our world in a better condition than we found it—in other words, capitalism that serves. And this is the hallmark of the inspiring leader—the leader who understands that the world serves us best when we serve it first. And the leader whose Destiny is to serve others and help them to grow and make the world a better place than they found it—is a leader who honors the sacredness of others.

The Concept of "Voice"

The notion of a "brand" is an important one for organizations and their products or services, and much good work has been done in this field. But the notion of a brand is a limiting idea. A larger, more inclusive concept is "voice." I define voice as "the experience a person *feels* when becoming conscious of a brand." It is the voice they "hear," which includes thousands of mental images, experiences, testimonials, and subconscious feelings. In a fraction of a second, the "voice" immediately repels or attracts. Every organization or product has a distinctive voice—the voice of Starbucks is different from the voice of Dunkin' Donuts, and the voice of Southwest Airlines is unlike that of American Airlines. What is arresting and inspiring in a powerful voice is how it serves, and, more importantly today, whether it serves a greater good—does it honor the sacredness of others? Does it make the world a better place?

Another component of voice is how well the needs of tradition, comfort, familiarity, and routine are served. If the voice offers a challenge to these, is something better being offered in their place?

Here is an example. The third most popular song in America (after *The Star Spangled Banner* and *Happy Birthday*) is *Take Me Out to the Ball Game,* in which the famous lines are traditionally sung in the seventh innings of baseball games:

Take me out to the ball game,
Take me out with the crowd;
Buy me some peanuts and Cracker Jack,
I don't care if I never get back.
Let me root, root, root for the home team,
If they don't win, it's a shame.
For it's one, two, three strikes, you're out,
At the old ball game.

Since the song was first penned in 1908, and despite several upgrades in health awareness over the last century, Cracker Jack remains a perennial favorite at all of the 30 Major League Baseball stadia in the United States, selling up to 1,000 bags at each game.

The voice of Cracker Jack is deeply ingrained in the psyche of millions of Americans. It is a strong voice, with a long history. First introduced in 1893 at Chicago's first World's Fair, by F.W. Rueckheim, it took three years for Louis Rueckheim, F.W.'s brother and partner, to discover how to keep the molasses-covered peanut and popcorn morsels from sticking together. When Louis invited a salesman to try some, he exclaimed, "That's crackerjack!" to which F.W. Rueckheim responded, "So it is," and so a registered trademark was born. With a gift in each bag, Cracker Jack is the world's largest user of toys and has produced enough of the product to circle the globe 69 times.

In 2004, the New York Yankees replaced Cracker Jack with another caramel corn, Crunch 'n Munch, but fans were furious and, using the twin arguments of ballpark tradition and the seventh-inning lyrics, demanded the restoration of Cracker Jack. After two months, management relented, and fans had their esteemed Cracker Jack back. "The fans have spoken," Yankees' chief operating officer, Lonn Trost, said at the time. Voice is a powerful force. A similar move a few years ago at Denver's Coors Field suffered the same fate. The voice of Cracker Jack resonated with fans more than the voice of Crunch'n Munch.

We typically buy products because they are good, or because the service is fantastic, or the habit of doing so feels comfortable, or because the price is right. That takes care of the intellectual reasons.

But there are other reasons, too, and they are far more subtle. One of them has to do with the subliminal and can be described loosely as *likeability*—the degree to which we like the company, its people, and what they stand for, and whether we are attracted to them, which is an essential part of an inspiring voice—in other words, if we feel served at the levels of both the social and the essentials selves.

Apple Inc. is a case in point. Its products are brilliant. Apple's products and services are not the lowest priced, but the "likeability index" for the company and its products is very strong. And Apple works carefully to grow this subliminal reputation and thus enhance its voice.

In 2009, Apple cancelled its membership in the United States Chamber of Commerce (USCC), the world's largest business federation, with three million members. Part of its resignation letter stated, "Apple is committed to protecting the environment and the communities in which we operate around the world. We strongly object to the Chamber's recent comments opposing the EPA's [Environmental Protection Agency] effort to limit greenhouse gases...As a company, we are working hard to reduce our own greenhouse emissions...We have undertaken this unilaterally and without government mandate, because we believe it is the right thing to do. For those companies who cannot or will not do the same, Apple supports regulating greenhouse gas emissions, and it is frustrating to find the Chamber at odds with us in this effort."

Apple has been joined by other high-profile defectors, including three utility companies, one of which, California's PG&E, announced it was leaving "because of the group's obstructionist tactics." Athletic wear company Nike had earlier resigned from the board of the USCC, declaring, "….we fundamentally disagree with the US Chamber of Commerce on the issue of climate change, and their recent action challenging the EPA is inconsistent with our view that climate change is an issue in need of urgent action…"

It takes courage to take a stand, but millions of people have noted this action by Apple, and the quality of Apple's voice and its "likeability index" will increase for many in their demographic market segment as a result. There are many ways to inspire the loyalty of customers and employees, and the integrity displayed by serving the greater good is one of the most powerful—and this builds the inspirational strength of an organization's voice.

Serving People Is Everyone's Job

Recently, I was asked if I knew anyone who could fill a position of Leadership and Organizational Development Consultant in a major corporation. The position description listed attributes such as the ability to serve others and guide them in the development of their leadership skills as the principal requirements. When we seek to populate organizations with a growing hierarchy of functional positions of this type, we are encouraging leaders to abdicate their responsibilities for learning and growing their passion for serving others. Transferring these leadership responsibilities to a cadre of specialists who are highly trained and skilled in the esoteric methodology of leadership development can mislead us into thinking that we have "fixed the problem." How wrong this is. We are each personally responsible for learning to become Higher Ground Leaders and serving and inspiring all those with whom we interact and all those who depend upon us and our integrity for the services they need, whether they are customers, employees, unions, suppliers, regulators, or the world in general. Specialists can be enormously helpful—even essential, because they teach us new ways of thinking and add strength to our strategies, and they have many valuable support roles to play— but serving those we lead, in the end, comes back to us.

A few days later, I was sitting with a senior executive whose company had recently been acquired by a giant multinational. She was describing how a set of faceless managers had descended on her organization and delivered an ultimatum requiring her to terminate half her employees, many of whom she had worked with closely for many years. Throwing them away like discarded pawns on a chessboard, although meeting certain financial conditions of the acquisition agreement, recognized no faces, no hearts, no souls, no compassion, but met another criteria—"getting the job done." In these circumstances, the metrics and the numbers do get met because fear and intimidation—the "old story" of leadership—prevail. But the people have not been served, and so the survivors dust off their résumés, update them, and scan alternative opportunities. The best talent is the most in demand, so they leave first, and while others may hang around longer, even they may eventually depart, leaving the company stripped of the asset that the acquirer should have valued most— its human spirits. While serving the employees of an acquired organization may seem like an obvious need, in so many acquisitions, the acquiring company mistakenly believes that it is buying physical assets and brand equity, when it is really acquiring the talents, gifts, and hearts of all the people who made the magic happen. Thinking we can keep the brand equity while eliminating the people who created it is the equivalent of banging one's head against the wall because it feels so good when you stop. Job one following an acquisition is serving the people who can realize the promise of the purchase.

As Franz Stigler, the World War II German fighter pilot, whose story you will read in Reflection Ten, said when asked why he didn't shoot in combat when he was up close, "When you can see the faces of people, you cannot shoot." When we see no faces, when we pass the problem of "resizing the organization" to another, such as an outplacement company, we abdicate our responsibilities and delude ourselves into believing that we have taken care of them, when what we have really done is let down the people who trusted us with their working lives.

The prevailing attitude of "old-story" leaders is *reactive negativism*—it's easier to say "no" than to do the hard work necessary to make a breakthrough in serving others. Recall how ATB made the practice of saying "yes" one of the paths to achieving their ONE Dream. That's why the first CASTLE Principle is Courage—it takes great and consistent courage to dismantle an entrenched system and to reinvent it so that others feel honored and respected, and therefore inspired. So, the lazy approach prevails: when sales slide, people are laid off; when margins slip, costs are slashed; when profits dip, training and benefits are frozen or withdrawn. Many practices that serve neither people nor the planet are left in place because it's easier to do so—because they do not require us to muster courage. I have even worked with leaders who have no appetite for changing broken practices because the problems, they say, will outlast their careers. When I asked the leader of one of the biggest banks in the country, employing more than 55,000 people, whether they were concerned that their staff turnover exceeded 28 percent, he replied, "No, it's about average for our industry." When I pointed out to him that one of our clients in the same industry had successfully lowered their staff turnover to 6 percent, he thought it was a fluke. Reactive acceptance of an annual cost of 15,000 employees who become so uninspired with their work that they decide to leave each year is unforgiveable. Fifteen thousand employees are being served so poorly by their leaders that they are choosing to leave in the hope of finding a more inspiring place to work. If replacements costs were only $25,000 per employee (and they are likely to be double that), then the annual cost to this bank—that is *every year*, not just one time—was $375 million!

This attitude costs America $147 billion each year in unnecessary staff turnover costs— it is the single largest avoidable corporate expense.

Staff turnover is one of the most important indicators of how well we are serving employees—even in industries that are notorious for high turnover. People stay with companies that serve and inspire them, and they leave companies that don't—it's as cut and dried as that.

Serving the Souls of Employees: Case Studies

Steven T. Bigari is a former McDonald's franchisee in Colorado Springs, Colorado, and a former "old-story" manager. He used to pay minimum wages to employees he recruited from the ranks of the working poor and routinely suffered annual staff turnover of 300 percent—the fast-food industry norm. To deal with shrinking profit margins, he implemented a traditional "old-story" plan: he cut employees' vacations. But during a conversation with his mentor, Brent Cameron, he had an epiphany, and reversed his thinking. He realized that if he put employees first, by serving them, they would take care of customers and build his business for him.

He dreamed up many creative ways to serve his employees— paying employees above the industry norm of minimum wage; working with a local church to arrange day-care; educating employees about public services available to low-wage workers; organizing transportation; making small, short-term, no-interest personal loans to his employees to help them pay their rent, buy tires, or meet other immediate needs. Over 10 years, only $900 was not repaid out of a total of $30,000 that Bigari loaned. Serving others, he discovered, was the key to inspiring them in an industry where employees missing their shifts and chronic staff turnover are a daily routine.

Because reliable transportation is such a challenge for minimum-wage workers, Steve Bigari would duck out of his restaurant during the busiest period—lunch hour on Saturdays—to look for cheap and dependable cars being sold at police auctions. Initially, he resold them at cost to his employees, then he experimented with renting them to his staff, and finally, he settled on collecting donated cars and selling them to a local dealer who would fix them up and resell them to employees.

Twenty-two-year-old Brettlyn O'Hara was living with her parents while earning about $800 a month working full-time at one of Bigari's McDonald's stores. She used to ride her bike or ask her parents for a ride to her job until she was able to use Bigari's program to buy a well-worn Oldsmobile Eighty-Eight sedan with 133,000 miles on the clock for $2,958. "It gets me into a car for a good monthly payment and helps me establish credit," said O'Hara. "The loan will help me get to a point where I can move out on my own." Bigari required employees who took out a loan to attend financial education courses and set aside $500 for maintenance and repairs. He realized that with an improved credit rating, employees would then be able to buy an even more reliable car within 18 months. Bigari financed 63 cars for employees in this way over a ten-year period, and he reflects today that only $960 went into default out of more than $500,000 in loans.

John Milliman and two associates from the University of Colorado were so intrigued by Bigari's service-to-employees approach that they conducted a research project into his practices. Their findings showed that from 2000 to 2002, staff turnover rates plunged at all of Bigari's restaurants—three even dropping below 100 percent—and in the same period, productivity rose, absenteeism fell, profit margins rose by more than three percentage points, and total profits increased by 11 percent. Employees utilizing these programs enthusiastically endorsed them, saying they helped to inspire them to achieve higher levels of performance.

Steve Bigari's attitude of serving employees first enabled him to build a highly successful McDonald's mini-empire of 12 stores, which he eventually sold to McDonald's and a former manager. (By then, staff turnover among his 440 employees had dropped to 74 percent—a remarkable accomplishment in the fast-food industry.) This enabled him to spend a year on a social entrepreneurship fellowship, before devoting himself fully to his ideas, which by now had been developed into a nonprofit organization, America's Family,[22] with backing from a venture philanthropy fund. America's Family aims "to empower working poor families with the tools, resources, and knowledge to gain financial self-sufficiency."

Employees yearn for many simple things in their work lives: to sleep in or come to work late; to leave early to attend to a family need; to work hours that suit personal schedules and requirements; to be rewarded and appreciated for results rather than time put in; to take advantage of the mobility and flexibility offered by modern technology; to integrate the best of both their work and personal lives; to practice hobbies and spend time with family before retiring—and yet, most of these are unavailable in "old-story" workplaces.

But Best Buy Co. is not an "old-story" company. At its Minneapolis, Minnesota, head office at 2 p.m. one afternoon, Chap Achen, who was head of the department that monitors everything that happens after someone places an online order with the company, stood up from his desk, closed his computer, and announced that he was finished for the day. "See you tomorrow. I'm going to a matinee," he said as he checked out to see a current hit movie. Elsewhere at Best Buy, Mark Wells was spending his daytime hours driving around the country attending Dave Matthews' rock concerts, and single mother Kelly McDevitt, an online promotions manager, was leaving at 2:30 p.m. to pick up

---

[22] www.amfol.com

her 11-year-old son Calvin from school, while Scott Jauman, a Six Sigma black belt, was spending a third of his time at his North Woods cabin.

To some, this might seem like anarchy. But it is a bold initiative by an enlightened company aimed at overcoming growing burnout, stress, workload pressures, and high staff turnover. The program is called ROWE (Results-only Work Environment), and its goal is to serve employees.

Four thousand of them at Best Buy no longer follow the antiquated, industrial-age requirement that equates physical presence with productivity. Gone are set hours, unnecessary meetings, long and numerous e-mails, schedules, mandatory meetings. Gone, too, is the political gamesmanship used to impress bosses about how hard someone is working. In the pre-ROWE days, Darrell Owens, a 14-year Best Buy veteran, once stayed up for three days in a row to complete a report. He was rewarded with a bonus and a vacation, but first, he says, "I ended up in the hospital." Another manager gave a plaque to an employee "who turns on the lights in the morning and turns them off at night."

Because results are the basis of rewards and performance evaluation, time or physical presence are now irrelevant. If you show up at the company's offices at 2 p.m., you are not late; and if you leave at that time, you're not leaving early, either. Time is irrelevant—results count. Says the program's co-founder, Jody Thompson, "This is like TiVo for your work."

Here is the formula: *Serving employees = higher performance.* Staff turnover in the online departments has declined by 90 percent, in logistics by 52 percent, and in sourcing by 75 percent. The average increase in employee productivity is 35 percent. Turnover amongst new employees during the first three months dropped from 14 percent to zero, job satisfaction rose 10 percent, and team performance scores rose 13 percent. In Chap Achen's department, orders processed by people who do not work in the office rose 13 to 18 percent compared to those who do. The Gap Outlet, a division of Gap Inc., is enrolling its 137 employees at corporate headquarters in San Francisco in a ROWE program, and the City of Minneapolis is supporting and encouraging companies along the overcrowded 35W corridor to follow suit, with the goal of reducing commuter traffic congestion.

Poor performers are exposed in this system because there is nowhere for shirkers to hide. Showing up is not work—it is the metric that "old-story" managers use to measure in an analogue age. But in the digital age, serving employees by offering them freedom, assisting them in the greater use of mobile technologies, empowering them, enabling them to adapt their schedules and lives so they can merge their personal needs with business objectives—these represent a sure path to their inspiration.

Best Buy employees say that their new freedom is changing their lives. They don't know if they work more or less hours, because they have stopped counting, but they are happier and more productive.

Organizations led by inspiring and inspired leaders *all* put employees before customers—a radical contradiction to the "old-story" the-customer-comes-first philosophy. It is no coincidence that top-performing organizations like Southwest Airlines, Starbucks, Pella Windows, Best Buy, FedEx, SAS Institute, TDIndustries, and Google, to name just a few, look upon their employees as their most important customers. Inspiring leadership is serving leadership—for employees first—and, of course, for everyone else, too.

> *Break your mirrors. Shatter the glass. In this self-absorbed society, look less at yourself and more at each other. Learn more about the face of your neighbor and less about your own.*
>
> Sargent Shriver

Reflection Nine: TRUTHFULNESS

[W]hen people thought the Earth was flat, they were wrong. When people thought the Earth was spherical, they were wrong. But if you think that thinking the Earth is spherical is just as wrong as thinking the Earth is flat, then your view is wronger than both of them put together.

Isaac Asimov

Why is truthfulness such an important and vital element of inspiring leadership? It is because we find the *experience* of interacting with a truthful person to be inspiring. The emotional and spiritual impact of a lie, or half-truth—the betrayal, dishonesty, and deception—is painful because it dishonors the sacredness of our relationships. The opposite is also true—it is not just the truth that we admire and that inspires us, but also the *courage* and *authenticity* behind it, because truthfulness is fueled by these two.

A lack of truthfulness or truth-telling—or, to be more precise, lying—is one of the most damaging forms of incivility, and incivility has a corrosive effect on others, whether they are friends, family, colleagues, business partners, or those we lead. Incivility is the direct opposite of honoring the sacredness of others. Christine Porath of the University of Southern California's Marshall School of Business and Christine Pearson of Thunderbird School of Global Management have polled several thousand managers and employees from a diverse range of United States companies over ten years about the impact of incivility on performance, and have found that of those experiencing incivility–

48 percent decreased their work effort;

47 percent decreased their time at work;

38 percent decreased their work quality;

66 percent said their performance declined;

80 percent lost work time worrying about the incident;

63 percent lost time avoiding the offender; and

78 percent said their commitment to the organization
declined.

We know from this and many other well-documented studies (and of course, our common sense), that lying, the mother of all uncivil behaviors, is unproductive—for performance, relationships, and employee and customer engagement—at home or work.

The practice of deceiving in communications, promotional programs, labeling, advertising, and customer service also corrodes the market as well as the workplace. Truthfulness and transparency are what makes a brand "sticky" for customers, yet they are often compromised in a process that entices customers to buy more stuff with more than $400 million in product and service rebates each year: industry experts estimate that 40 percent of these rebates remain unredeemed, putting $2 billion dollars of extra revenue into the pockets of retailers and their suppliers. Some of this is simply due to people's forgetfulness. But a lot of it is caused by the restrictions, complexity, and hurdles faced by customers when they attempt to redeem their rebate; a short-term gain for the seller, but a long-term grievance and resentment for the customer—a broken trust, and a diminishing of the organization's voice. Weighing up the odds of this bet, truthfulness wins hands down—for those who refuse to grasp a short-term gain at the expense of the long term.

Finding Our Way Again

We are born truthful. Then we begin a journey where some lose the script.

The 2009 Junior Achievement/Deloitte Teen Ethics Survey

found that 71 percent of teens feel fully prepared to make ethical decisions in the workplace, but nearly 40 percent of them believe that lying, cheating, plagiarizing, and violence are sometimes necessary to succeed in school, and half (49 percent) say that lying to parents or guardians is okay—with 61 percent admitting to having done so in the last year.

Less than half (49 percent) of these young respondents say that they look to their parents as role models, and many have no role models at all. Consequently perhaps, teens feel "more accountable" to themselves (86 percent) than they do to their parents or guardians (52 percent), their friends (41 percent), or society (33 percent).

Reflect on what this data tells us. They didn't make this stuff up—someone had to teach, coach, and lead them into believing they could accommodate the contradictions, "Yes, I make ethical decisions," and "Yes, I lie, cheat, and defraud." If our leaders teach children a moral relativism that accommodates deceit, corner-cutting, and spin, our children will bring this lack of moral clarity to their future roles as leaders, too.

Not only is it vital that we show others the incongruity of saying, "Yes, I'm an ethical leader," and in the next breath saying, "Yes, I break rules," but, as leaders, it is our role to model the way of a Higher Ground Leader—congruity, integrity, and truthfulness.

Lying: The Result of Personal Cynicism

Says Lucy Kellaway, a management columnist for the *Financial Times*, "I am a liar. This statement doesn't sound pretty, but it's the truth. So far today, I've congratulated someone on their new job, even though I think it a complete mystery how they ever got promoted. I e-mailed various readers thanking them for their interesting points, which I actually thought were tedious.

"If you work in an organization, I'd bet my shirt that you are a liar, too. We're all liars, but lies are necessary. The corporate world demands them. Indeed, it cannot function without them.

"There are loads of reasons for this. Workplaces are hierarchies. That means we kiss up and kick down. Offices are competitive, which means putting your best foot forward and selling yourself. Which usually means stretching the truth.

"The rules of office life also invite workers to cover up any infringements. So we lie about taking days off, being late for work, or slacking. Unrealistic targets and budgets also make lying essential. In fact, lying about the work itself is necessary to keep us doing it. Thus, we claim to be 'passionate' about what we do, when in fact we barely tolerate it."

This is a sad commentary for two reasons: first, it comes from a source that is respected and influential, sets standards of leadership behavior, and purports to provide cutting-edge thinking about business. Second, it is so cynical that it is deeply depressing, missing by a wide mark the inspiration and honoring of each other that most people so long for. Worse, it encourages the dishonoring behavior and lower standards we abhor.

Often, leaders who fall into the habit of using dishonest jargon do so because they are simply blind to the damage it causes. A euphemism, designed to "spin" the truth, is one of the subtlest and most insidious forms of lying. When Nokia Siemens Networks laid off 9,000 employees, they issued a press release describing the action as a "synergy-related headcount adjustment goal." Deceptive bafflegab like this demoralizes followers and undermines the credibility of leaders because it violates *all* of the CASTLE Principles, including Truthfulness. Uninspiring organizations accept and condone this form of weasel-worded language as standard practice in the mistaken belief that it makes the action appear to be more noble: eBay's CFO described the discarding of 1,600 employees as "actions to simplify our organization," and other firms resort to slippery pseudo-truths such as, "reduction in force (RIF)," "offboarding," "rationalizing," "surplussing," "de-verticalization," "strategic review of strategies," and "restructuring." As Alfred North Whitehead reminded us,

"There are no whole truths: all truths are half-truths. It is trying to treat them as whole truths that plays the devil."

I have noticed that, in organizations, the mere commitment to becoming a band of truth-tellers leads to a sharp increase in morale, employee and customer engagement and satisfaction, performance, and inspiration. The commitment to kick it up a notch—to Higher Ground Leadership—by rededicating ourselves to truth-telling, boosts self-esteem and is deeply inspiring because it raises our pride in our colleagues. We know we stand for something that is above average and noble. Because the demand for truth always exceeds the supply, a commitment to truthfulness is a simple approach to moving the inspiration needle in organizations and a sure way for each of us to return to the script. As Albert Schweitzer said, "Truth has no special time of its own. Its hour is now—always." We *love* and admire people who tell the truth, because we respect their authenticity, morality, and desire to honor the sacredness of others—and few fail to be inspired by such behavior.

As leaders, those we lead quite rightly expect us to model the standards we expect from them. We may exhort our employees to speak the truth, but if we "spin" the truth, we have no right to expect anything better than the shabby standards we have ourselves established. When we raise the bar, setting a higher standard of truthfulness, we introduce a new level of excitement and inspiration, because we inspire the hope in others that we are creating a community of truth-tellers, that we honor the sacredness of the truth, and that we are striving to be Higher Ground Leaders. It represents the signal that followers are waiting for—that something better lies ahead. And that is inspiring.

Anatomy of a Decision Point

Often when we are faced with a challenge—a decision point—our natural reaction is to hunker down and hope that bombast and denial will tide us over until the challenge passes. This is the exact moment when followers most earnestly look to their leaders for cues about the strength of their integrity. Will the essential self or the social self determine the actions taken? Will the leader be true to his or her North Star? Will the leader's Why-Be-Do guide the next steps? Will the action, policy, or decision be inspiring? Will this leader represent a flame that inspires me?

Bill Hawkins says that the purpose of Medtronic, the $15-billion Minneapolis-based medical device maker, "To alleviate pain and to extend life," is something he takes very seriously. Two months after he took over as CEO, Hawkins faced a decision point. He had completed a very successful road show with investors and analysts explaining his vision for the future and the benefits of a recent acquisition. His buoyancy was punctured when the president of the cardiac rhythm business came up to him and said, "I need to speak with you." He had data regarding one of Medtronic's products, the Sprint Fidelis, indicating that its rate of resistance to fractures was 99.1 percent compared to 99.7 for other Medtronic leads. Though not statistically significant, this, together with a report from a hospital stating it had observed a higher-than-expected fracture rate, suggested that the Sprint Fidelis might not perform well over time.

Leads are super-thin, insulated wires connecting an implanted defibrillator to heart muscles which signal the device to emit a life-saving shock to the heart, and Sprint Fidelis was Medtronic's latest, featherweight model. Fractured leads are dangerous because the patient can be subjected to random, unnecessary shocks, or, just as dangerous, none when they are vitally needed.

Medtronic had been monitoring a few cases where a lead malfunction might have played a role in the death of a patient. So two months into his new role, Bill Hawkins faced a dramatic decision point. Recalling the product could send his company's share price and revenues into a tailspin. Besides, a recall of defibrillators involves removing implanted devices from patients—not a simple process, since there were already 25,000 patients wearing them. If he hunkered down and used flimflam, bombast, and denial, he'd be gambling Medtronic's stellar reputation, damage the company's "voice," and, worst of all, endanger the lives of patients. Said Hawkins at the time, "It was a rough way to start."

Hawkins convened a group of internal experts, as well as an independent advisory board of physicians practicing separately from Medtronic, to assess the facts. The conclusion was that there was no evidence that the lead should be removed from the market, but that the company should closely watch the situation.

Medtronic monitors device implants using radio technology embedded in the devices that communicates to a Web server, and they wrote a specific program to monitor the performance of the 25,000 implanted Sprint Fidelis devices to see if there were any signs that these leads might have a higher risk of fracture.

Bill Hawkins recalls that three days later, on Sunday afternoon, he drove his children to church and then sat in his car for 90 minutes in the church parking lot while participating in a conference call with his advisors and colleagues. Hawkins dug deep—he summoned his essential self and reflected on the sacredness of Medtronic's corporate culture: "to alleviate pain, restore health, and extend life." He wanted to get the decision right, and, whatever that turned out to be, implement it in a timely way. On that conference call, he and his colleagues decided to voluntarily suspend shipments and take the Sprint Fidelis off the market. The team set a timetable of five business days to prepare for a public announcement.

Once committed to a path of truthfulness and transparency, Medtronic embarked on five frenzied days of activity: materials were prepared for physicians around the world; letters were readied for doctors, patients, and regulatory authorities; the FDA was briefed (who agreed that Medtronic was doing the right thing); Medtronic's media relations department briefed the *New York Times*, the *Wall Street Journal*, and other papers with information under embargo; a group of outside physicians was organized to help the media understand the issue; a Web-based information session was arranged for the sales team, so they could contact their customers personally, to avoid surprises.

Hawkins called both of Medtronic's major competitors; one did not return his call, the other did, and Hawkins alerted him about the forthcoming announcement.

The following Monday, the company went live, with Hawkins making the announcement, following which he immediately flew to a board meeting. Despite the impact of the decision, Hawkins received the full endorsement of the board, who told him that this decision point, and Hawkins' display of integrity and truth-telling, was the perfect way for them to assess the quality of a new CEO.

There are trade-offs in situations like this. Medtronic took a significant financial hit following their announcement—shares plunged 12 percent—the worst day's trading for the company in 23 years. Almost 63 million shares changed hands on announcement day, compared to 3.6 million the day before, and in the year after the recall, Medtronic's market share fell from 51 percent to 47 percent.

On the other hand, their voice was enhanced, they did the right thing and operated with transparency, and, in time, strengthened their reputation for integrity and restored their leadership position in the industry. Medtronic developed a software package, the Lead Integrity Alert, approved by the FDA, that issues an alert to patients if unstable performance by the lead is detected. Medtronic is thus able to monitor the leads more closely and intervene earlier, providing greater confidence to patients and reducing the chances of complications. In Medtronic's case, as in many others, authenticity and truthfulness can be expensive in the short term. But in the long term, doing the right thing and protecting the "voice" of an organization is far more important.

Bill Hawkins led from Higher Ground. He consulted with his colleagues and objective outsiders and briefed his board, the analysts, and the markets—even his competitors—so they would not be blindsided. He made the right decision, even though the statistical evidence was "not significant," and in doing so, set a high standard for truthfulness, which inspired many.

To paraphrase Ralph Waldo Emerson, in the corporate world, and in our roles as leaders in all aspects of our lives, the greatest homage we can pay to truth is to use it.

In a time of universal deceit, telling the truth becomes a revolutionary act.

George Orwell

Reflection Ten: LOVE

Water is fluid, soft, and yielding. But water will wear away rock, which is rigid and cannot yield. As a rule, whatever is fluid, soft, and yielding will overcome whatever is rigid and hard. This is another paradox: what is soft is strong.

Lao-Tzu

If you don't believe that we should love all others—what exactly do you believe?

If you believe that love is an emotion we reserve for our loved ones and friends and is not a "business subject," how do you justify that?

Love is to the soul what food is to the body. Love is a noble act that serves others, offering respect, openness, trust, and loyalty. The more we love, the more we lose the ego-part of ourselves, and yet, in doing so, we don't become less in any way, but instead, one with those we love.

Love—the Word and the Inspiration

In the Anglo-Saxon tradition, there is a very uneasy relationship with the word love. There are 96 words for love in the Sanskrit-based languages, 80 in Persian, 3 in Greek, and 1 in English. And yet, we all yearn to be loved—even when we are not always easy to love. Since the need to be loved is so strong for us all, it is important to realize that we cannot expect to receive what we are not prepared to give. It is through being a loving person that we become an inspiring leader.

As Paul McCartney reminds us, "And, in the end, the love you take / Is equal to the love you make."

We are surrounded by inspiring people—they are everywhere—and they are all that way because they choose love over fear and intimidation. Think of those you know who are inspiring—they love you. It is the love within their hearts that inspires you. And they are that way, even when they don't feel like it, or when their circumstances might seem to dictate the opposite.

How Love Won in War

In June of 1990, a hotel lobby in Seattle was the scene of an extraordinary meeting between two unique men. Two fighter airplane aces, foes decreed by war 50 years ago, had flown close enough to each other to allow brief visual contact between them, but they had never actually looked each other in the eye, shaken each other's hand, or, as they were now doing, given each other a big bear hug. There was an immediate, heartfelt rapport between them as they took the elevator up to a room on the third floor to recall the event that was so vividly etched into their minds that one of them still had recurring nightmares about it, and yet the experience still seemed so surreal that they sometimes doubted its occurrence. Settling into the well-upholstered armchairs in the hotel room, and with drinks in hand to facilitate their conversation, they became brothers of choice as they helped each other piece together an incredible puzzle that would tell a remarkable story of chivalry and fear-transcending human love.

On December 20, 1943, a cold and wintry day, Charles L. Brown of the 379th Bomb Group lined up his B-17F for takeoff. He was just 21. Commencing his very first combat mission, he had no awareness about how soon the grace of love would plead with fate to save his life and the lives of his crew members. His plane, whimsically named Ye Olde Pub, was scheduled to take part in the bombing of an FW-190 factory in Bremen, Germany.

As Charlie Brown began his bomb run at 23,000 feet, he immediately encountered heavy and accurate flak as he flew through airstreams registering a frigid minus 60 degrees Fahrenheit. His plane was barraged with a series of severe hits, which knocked out two of its engines, damaged a third, and hobbled his B-17, reducing it to just one engine at full power. The aircraft's compass, controls, oxygen, and hydraulic and electrical systems were all damaged.

The pilot and crew received serious wounds, too—a bullet fragment pierced Charlie Brown's right shoulder, while all but one of his comrades were so severely wounded that they could no longer defend themselves or their plane. "They beat us up quite badly," Brown told me. "As I was struggling along, all of a sudden, I looked up and there were eight FW-190s to my right lining up to attack."

As he weighed his rapidly dwindling options, Charlie Brown decided to go on the offensive, using his weakened firepower against the waves of oncoming fighter planes, but, struggling with his injury and starved of oxygen, Brown was unable to sustain his defenses. He remembers becoming inverted after recovering from a steep turn and "looking up" at the ground before passing out. Regaining consciousness, he found the aircraft miraculously flying straight and level, but perilously low—below 1,000 feet.

"When you experience anoxia [a severe deficiency of oxygen in the body]," Brown explained to me, "you have absolutely no memory of what you were doing. The world stops—and it starts. And your memory picks up where the world starts again."

Dropping down from this aerial skirmish, World War II German fighter ace Oberleutnant L. Franz Stigler landed to refuel and rearm when he saw Brown's B-17 emerging from behind a wooded area across the field where he was refueling. Stigler, sensing his third "kill" of the day, sprinted for his plane and jumped into his cockpit, taking off in hot pursuit. Flying at 500 feet above the enemy aircraft, he considered how best to finish it off.

"I thought I would do it the classic way, from the rear," remembered Stigler. "So, I flew above and to the rear of the airplane, about 200 feet. I wanted to give his tail-gunner a chance to lift the guns, to point the guns at me. The guns were hanging down."

But the guns didn't lift and Stigler, flying within 20 feet, suddenly realized why. Blood was running down the barrels. "I saw his gunner lying in the back profusely bleeding...so, I couldn't shoot." He then maneuvered alongside the stricken plane's right wing and peered into the cockpit at Brown. "I tried to get him to land in Germany, and he didn't respond at all." Stigler realized that Brown's lack of reaction was due, in part, to his lack of oxygen. As Stigler peered into the aircraft, he could see the crew members frantically treating the wounded and realized that shooting down the aircraft in this condition would be like shooting men in their parachutes. "So, I figured, well, turn him to Sweden, because his airplane was so shot up; I never saw anything flying so shot up."

Though partially dazed, Charlie Brown was concerned for his severely injured comrades on board and therefore rejected the possibility of bailing out or crash-landing. Using the one remaining engine, he edged the battered bomber in a climb, pursuing the risky gamble of reaching the United Kingdom.

And as he did so, glancing out of his right window, he spotted Stigler's Bf-109 flying tight on his wing. Alarmed and struggling to control his badly damaged plane, Brown observed the Bf-109 pilot wave, then fly across the B-17's nose. The pilot signaled for him to land in Germany, but Charlie Brown refused. In an extraordinary act of combat chivalry, the Luftwaffe pilot changed tack, escorting Ye Olde Pub for several miles across the North Sea towards England before saluting, soaring into the grey North Atlantic cloud cover, and returning to Europe.

After a harrowing flight across 250 inhospitable miles of the North Sea, Charlie landed his bedraggled bomber safely at Seething, near the English coast.

Who was this mysterious Luftwaffe pilot who gallantly spared

Charlie and his comrades? Why had he not completed the mission he had begun, by destroying the plane? These questions would haunt Charles Brown for nearly 50 years before they were answered.

After landing, Lieutenant Brown and his crew were debriefed regarding their mission. He was interrogated about his unusual encounter with the Bf-109. This debriefing was classified "secret" and was embargoed for many years. Charles Brown later completed a combat tour, finished college, accepted a regular commission, and served in the Office of Special Investigations with the Joint Chiefs of Staff and in other Air Force and State Department assignments. He retired to Miami, Florida, where he founded an energy conservation and environmental research center specializing in combustion research.

Forty-three years later, Brown decided to unlock his wartime enigma and find the chivalrous Luftwaffe pilot who had spared his plane and the lives of his crew. In 1990, almost four years after his search began, Charlie Brown received a letter from former Oberleutnant Franz Stigler in response to a notice published in a newsletter for German fighter pilots. Stigler was by then living in Surrey, British Columbia, Canada. Brown called him and during their phone conversation, the two men compared notes, including time, place, and aircraft markings, and eventually confirmed their extraordinary first meeting in the sky nearly half a century before.

Stigler had enjoyed a celebrated Luftwaffe career: in his 487 combat missions in the Bf-109, he had 28 confirmed victories and was wounded 4 times. He finished the war flying 16 more combat missions in the ME-262 jet, assigned to the select JV-44, the celebrated Squadron of Experts (Aces), making him one of the world's earliest jet fighter pilots in combat. Stigler's decision to spare Charlie Brown's B-17 was even more remarkable considering that in Nazi Germany, such an act would subject Stigler to a court-martial which, if he were found guilty, could have cost him his life. Brown was lucky indeed—previously on that day in

December 1943, Stigler had already downed two four-engine bombers and could have earned a Knight's Cross, the highest German Luftwaffe honor, by shooting down one more. But when he saw the human and pitiful condition of the plane and its wounded crew, he felt emotionally unable to carry out the sinister duty required by the rules of war. Instead, he followed the call of love to reprieve, as he would later say, "the most heavily damaged aircraft I ever saw that was still flying."

"Franz came up to within 20 feet of our tail," Brown recalls. "He could see that our tail-gunner was dead, and he could see the blood running down the gun barrels." Stigler later shared with Brown that his decision not to fire at the B-17 was heavily influenced by the fact that, as Brown told me, "he saw men, and he had never fired at men before; he had always fired at airplanes. Not only did he see men, he saw helpless men." Charles Brown believed that Stigler's early training in a monastery from age 8 to 16 was likely a contributing factor in his being able to see the people, rather than just the plane, and allowing compassion to guide his action, even though it could have cost him his life.

From their reunion in the Seattle hotel in 1990 until Franz Stigler passed away on March 22, 2008, the two remained close friends. "To say that there was a lot of love between us is an understatement," Brown told me. Stigler's obituary referred to Brown as "special brother Charlie Brown." The online guestbook honoring Stigler contained many entries from people he had never known but who had heard about him and felt compelled to acknowledge this extraordinary Luftwaffe pilot and his selfless act of chivalry and love. One entry read: "Franz...you showed us all that the love for each other we have as human beings is far more powerful than war."

In 2008, more than 60 years after Brown safely landed his badly damaged B-17 on the British coast, wounded crew on board, he was awarded the Air Force Cross, the second highest military decoration that can be awarded to a member of the

United States Air Force. Since the time it was first awarded in 1962, there have been less than 200 recipients of this distinguished medal. But prior to accepting the medal, Brown wanted to ensure recognition for his crew. He nominated each of them for the Silver Star and felt satisfied when the award was granted, even though only three crew members were still alive at the time.

The Mighty Eighth Air Force Museum in Savannah, Georgia, took interest in the decisive encounter between Charlie Brown's B-17 and Franz Stigler's Bf-109 (also known as Me-109), and in 2000, both men met at the museum, commemorating their visit by donating signed lithographs of themselves as World War II pilots. An exhibit at the museum features the encounter as a teaching model in the Character Education programs for the State of Georgia. The Mighty Eighth Air Force Museum is a designated Center for Character Education, in which all students from kindergarten through high school are required to participate. The programs focus on twenty-seven character traits, with "Compassion" being the trait said to have been demonstrated by Franz Stigler in sparing the lives of Charlie Brown and his crew.

In this remarkable story, we learn that at our core, we are not natural killers or warriors. It is hard for us to be brutal or unloving when, as Franz Stigler observed, we see into the faces of real people. It is easier to "kill" a plane than a human spirit. In James Cameron's film *Avatar,* the Na'vi people of the planet Pandora greet each other with the words, "I see you." This is much more than a formality. When they say this to another person, it is an acknowledgment that they see the other as being like themselves, that they honor the sacredness of the other, that they understand that they are one, and that what they do to the other, they do to themselves. In our world, the Sanskrit greeting *Namaste* holds a similar meaning. It acknowledges that the "I" and the "you" that we represent are the same—part of a bigger whole. Even if we find ourselves—metaphorically or literally—embroiled in a violent path that we did not choose, we still have the option of honoring the sacred in the other, and therefore to love them.

We do not inspire through fear or warrior behavior; we inspire through our loving relationships with others. The mentors, coaches, parents, and teachers who inspired us have all taught us this lesson.

Being Strong Enough to Be Gentle

For all our bravado, and the legacy of learning about warrior leadership, we are now realizing that greatness and inspiration come from love, not war; from compassion and empathy, not victory, violence, and domination. Our "old-story" model of leadership is evolving quickly: the ruthless, ambitious, hard-charging A-type achiever is giving way to the "New Story"—the caring, listening, mentoring leader who yearns to make the world a better place and to serve. It is unnatural for us to live out our lives as pseudo-warriors. Our essential self is comprised of the yin and the yang, the feminine as well as the masculine energies, and suppressing either one contravenes the desire of the soul. Fear and violence—the yang energy—can move us to action. But love—the yin energy—inspires. From Zorro to Zen.

Love is the magician that pulls man out of his own hat.

Ben Hecht

Reflection Eleven: EFFECTIVENESS

*People, like nails, lose their effectiveness when they
lose direction and begin to bend.*

Walter Savage Landor

We tend to think of effectiveness as something we "do" to people. But in fact it is who we "are," not what we do, that changes the world and people around us. As the Greek author Plutarch wrote, "What we achieve inwardly will change outer reality."

It is important here to distinguish between efficiency and effectiveness. In the words of Grace Hopper, "Efficiency tends to deal with Things. Effectiveness tends to deal with People. We manage Things, we lead People." We all wish to be effective in our lives. In our work with Higher Ground Leadership, we define "effective" this way: "Achieving desired outcomes successfully"—to reach the goals we have set for ourselves, whether on the spiritual, mental, or physical levels.

Effectiveness is both a cause and a result. We are the most effective when we have learned to be courageous, authentic, serving, truthful, and loving—when we have fully integrated the first five CASTLE Principles into our lives, and are *living* them. When these attributes have become part of who we are and how we live and lead others, and if we then follow our North Star from that sacred place, Effectiveness is the natural and inevitable consequence. It is inevitable because we are inspired—and therefore inspiring.

Inspiration Is the Source of Exceptional Effectiveness

Inspiration and effectiveness always wax and wane together—both the quality and quantity of output are directly influenced by our level of inspiration at any given time.

Giacomo Puccini said, "Inspiration is an awakening, a quickening of all man's faculties, and it is manifested in all high artistic achievements." And all work is art.

In their peak years, the Beatles were an extraordinarily effective and powerful force. Hardly any sacrifice was too great in their quest for effectiveness—they would sleep in the studio, work through the night—whatever it took to create and record their music and meet studio deadlines. In just one year, for example, 1965, the film *Help* was released, along with 14 songs, including the hits *Help, You've Got to Hide Your Love Away, You're Going to Lose That Girl, Ticket to Ride, I've Just Seen a Face*, and *Yesterday*. But this inspired quartet was in pursuit of their Calling and their year was just warming up. After completing an eleven-date run in the last two weeks of August, including a record-breaking attendance at New York's Shea Stadium, the Beatles wrote and recorded 14 new songs in 30 days for their next album, *Rubber Soul*. Many of these songs, such as *Drive My Car, Norwegian Wood, Nowhere Man, Michelle, Girl, I'm Looking Through You*, and *In My Life*, still stand out as pop classics to this day—half a century later—showcasing brilliant levels of creativity and innovation, fresh melodies and lyrics, manipulation of tapes to achieve different or new effects, and novel use of instrumentation, such as the sitar in *Norwegian Wood* and the harpsichord effect in *In My Life*. Before August was over (remember, this was the age of 45 rpm discs), the band had produced two more songs that became a double-sided hit single—*We Can Work It Out* and *Day Tripper*. Sixteen published and recorded songs in 30 days! And their pursuit of effectiveness—the quest for *exactly* the result they were looking for, knew no bounds. To get their song *I Will* just right, the Beatles recorded it 65 times.

The beating heart of effectiveness is the inspiration that comes from a deep inner awareness of one's *Why-Be-Do*—our North Star—tempered by the CASTLE Principles and a prodigious commitment to excellence. This effectiveness, at its very highest levels, is sometimes referred to as genius. But as Buckminster Fuller reminded us, "Everyone is born a genius, but the process of living de-geniuses them."

Elegance and Grace

The beautiful thing about all this is that it requires no contrary effort—no effort that requires us to "push against" something—just the wisdom to follow the natural energy of what we know to be right. And it will work best for us when we listen—truly listen—to our inner voices and follow the sometimes counterintuitive paths we are being asked to take: what we earlier defined as authenticity. The path to effectiveness is straightforward, logical, elegant, and graceful. I have summarized and defined the components as follows:

The Essentials of Effectiveness
- There is nothing to learn, only old habits to break and original qualities to restore.
- There is nothing complicated here—it is so simple that it is almost absurd. Remember, the word being used here is *simple* —and that does not necessarily mean *easy*.
- The old adage is, "If it ain't broke, don't fix it." But in this case, the opposite is more likely to be true: if it feels boring and uninspiring, it may not be working as effectively as it could, and therefore it may be time to retire the old model and replace it with a new one.
- If it is negative in any way—ugly, dirty, noisy, unappealing,

complicated, harmful, hurtful, dangerous, environmentally destructive, or dishonest—it is bound to fail. This is so because negative energy is a signal that we are "forcing" something unnaturally. If it is elegant and graceful, it is bound to succeed, because the default center point of life rests in elegance and grace.

- If it is uninspiring, it is going to be harder to achieve; make it inspiring—the natural energy towards completion will then flow your way.
- If it affronts the soul, it will fail. Honor the sacredness of the other, respect the concept of oneness, and alignment of interests and purpose will follow.

It takes the effort of negative energy to oppose the CASTLE Principles—to be cowardly, duplicitous, selfish, dishonest, aggressive, or incompetent, and especially to be profane. And the opposite is true—pouring our energy into being courageous, authentic, serving, truthful, loving, and effective yields the outcomes and the sacredness we yearn for. Pouring our energy into the clarity and purity of our *Why-Be-Do* is also the most effective way to live our lives and get things done.

Effectiveness Is the Sum of Many Small Actions

Sometimes, we have a tendency to think small, as if the world were too big for it to be affected by our puny efforts. Such thinking is the enemy of effectiveness because it is often self-fulfilling. We are not small or insignificant, but powerful beyond our imagination. Buckminster Fuller, famed architect, author, designer, futurist, inventor, and visionary, said, "I always say to myself: What is the most important thing we can think about at this extraordinary moment?" In a February 1972 interview with *Playboy*'s Barry Fuller, Buckminster Fuller said, "Something hit me very hard once, thinking about what one little man could do. Think of the Queen Mary—the whole ship goes by and then comes the rudder.

And there's a tiny thing at the edge of the rudder called a trim tab. It's a miniature rudder. Just moving the little trim tab builds a low pressure that pulls the rudder around. Takes almost no effort at all. So I said that the little individual can be a trim tab. Society thinks it's going right by you, that it's left you altogether. But if you're doing dynamic things mentally, the fact is that you can just put your foot out like that and the whole big ship of state is going to go. So I said, 'Call me Trimtab.'"

In the period leading up to his death, Buckminster Fuller's wife had been lying comatose in a Los Angeles hospital, dying of cancer. It was while visiting her there that he exclaimed, at a certain point: "She is squeezing my hand!" He then stood up, suffered a heart attack, and died an hour later. Chiseled into Buckminster Fuller's gravestone at Cambridge, Massachusetts, are the words: *Call me Trimtab*.

Unlearning Is a Precondition for Effectiveness

Many people find it hard to believe that making a breakthrough that leads to a significant increase in effectiveness can be achieved quickly. People often take me aside and quietly ask me to share the "secret sauce" that I teach clients—in skiing and in leadership. But, in both environments, I tell them, "You're asking the wrong question. You see, it's not so much about what we need to learn; it's more about what we need to *unlearn*."

On February 12, 1995, the *New York Times* broke a story about the Swedish government's embarrassing admission that their defense forces had been blowing up minks and seals instead of Russian submarines in their coastal waters. The *Times* quoted Prime Minister Ingvar Carlsson as saying, "It's a sad fact that what was originally stated to be intrusions into our waters, have proved to be minks."

Beginning in the mid-1970s—the hair-trigger, paranoid, cold-war years—the Swedish defense forces began hunting submarines in the fjords and islands of Sweden, Norway, and Finland, a sensitive buffer zone between the former communist Soviet Union and the West. Depth charges and grenades were dropped, and remote-controlled mines detonated in dozens of forays each year—always during the warmer months. A spokesperson reported that, on one occasion, "the prowler was detected and trapped in 282 feet of water...about 60 miles south of Stockholm," but, as in every other case, the submarines evaded their pursuers, slipping away amidst the ensuing confusion and turbulence.[23] In October 1981, Swedish suspicions were augmented when a Soviet submarine made a navigation error, becoming stranded on rocks near a military base at Karlskrona. The submarine was a diesel-powered vessel of the type called Whiskey class by NATO.

Many theories abounded: the Soviets were seeking hiding places for future warfare; the Soviets were testing their submarines' evasion techniques; the Soviets were probing Swedish antisubmarine defenses. The repeated denials by the Soviets of their submarines' presence in Swedish territorial waters simply heightened the Swedes' suspicions. In 1982, Rear Admiral Per Rudbeck declared, "a foreign power is preparing for war against us."

In February of 1995, Owe Wiktorin, Supreme Commander of Sweden's armed services, revealed Sweden's faux pas while presenting a report about his country's military and naval activity. He said that through the use of new hydrophonic measuring instruments, it had been shown that sounds that had long been identified as coming from foreign submarines could actually be traced to minks, which had similar sound patterns. He concluded that, since 1992 at least, there had been no intrusions by Soviet submarines into Sweden's territorial waters.

Even though the possibility that the Swedish Navy might be pursuing playful minks and seals had been suggested as early as

---

[23] Starbuck, William, H., "Unlearning Ineffective Behavior or Obsolete Technologies," *International Journal of Technology Management*, 1996, 11: 725-737; and *The New York Times*, Sunday, February 12, 1995, section 1, page 10, New York edition

1987, the Swedish military brass had fallen back on their old knowledge, beliefs, and detection techniques. When Tero Harkonen, a Swedish seal expert, first suggested that the navy's anti-submarine response had been tripped by young seals playing, his findings were dismissed. "They can play, gush through the water, and even create foam on the surface," he tried to explain, but navy officials insisted that they had seen the bubbles of divers and had corralled a foreign mini-submarine or another type of underwater vessel with their nets. They justified their erroneous assessment by pointing to the many "reliable" sightings of suspected alien submarines and submarine activity in the area over the preceding two months. Even after the mink-and-seal theory was raised, the Swedish Navy continued searching and dropping depth charges for ten more days before abandoning the exercises.

When we are frightened, or when we begin calcifying our beliefs or attitudes, we resort to the familiar, and close our minds. When this happens, new learning is impossible, and effectiveness is seriously impaired. An intermediate skier, faced with a cliff and a 60-degree pitch, will resort to old, defensive habits—a *snow plow* (a maneuver in which the skis are wedged to slow down speed) or *side-slipping* (a technique where the skis are angled at 90 degrees to the incline of the slope to slow or avert descent). Defensive approaches are chosen when we experience fear. Advanced skiers, on the other hand, would approach such a challenge by choosing *offensive* techniques based on courage and commitment. But to do so effectively, they must first set aside old methods and habits, and this is difficult to do without a trusted teacher—someone who can inspire the confidence required to overcome the fear associated with the challenge. At first glance, skiing down the cliff may seem terrifying. However, if the descent is broken into three pieces—tight turns for the steepest first third, wider turns for the less steep middle third, and carving turns for the ski-out, for example, it becomes manageable.

Unlearning, then, is a prerequisite for effectiveness, which leads to growth. We see the world not as it is, but as we would like it to be, and unlearning is like seeing the world with new eyes. The steps to unlearning are:

1. Admit that an old practice, belief, or attitude is not solving the current challenge and is no longer serving you, and therefore doing more of it will not lead to the desired outcomes.
2. Open your mind. Yield to the view that there are alternatives to the way you have "always done it" until now.
3. Switch from trying to rationalize the use of your long-favored solution, to asking questions about how you can change, learn, and grow.
4. Commit to terminating the old way—forever. This is the toughest part.
5. Practice and perfect the new way. This is the easiest part.

That's the "secret sauce." As Satchel Paige said, "It's not what you don't know that hurts you; it's what you know that just ain't so."

Reframing

A wise farmer owned a prize horse, but one day it ran away. The neighbors came to see him and commiserate. "Isn't it a terrible thing that your horse ran away?" they all said.

The farmer said, "Maybe yes, maybe no."

The next day, the horse returned, with a filly in tow. The neighbors came to visit again and declared, "How lucky you are that that your horse came back and brought a beautiful filly with him!"

The farmer said, "Maybe yes, maybe no."

The next day, the farmer's son was training the filly, but when it threw him, he fell and broke his leg. Once again the neighbors offered up their opinion, "Isn't it a tragedy that your son broke his leg? Now he can't help you with your farming projects until he is well again. That's just a shame!"

The farmer said, "Maybe yes, maybe no."

The next day, the Emperor paid an unexpected visit to con-script all the young men for his latest war. But because the farmer's son's leg was broken, they allowed him to remain on the farm. The neighbors, ever ready to pass judgment, said, "How fortunate that your son had a broken leg. This saved him from having to risk his life in the war!"

The farmer said, "Maybe yes, maybe no..."

How we see things depends upon our experience, our habits of perception (negative, positive, cynical, optimistic, etc.) and, most of all, our choices. We can hand over choice to fate, or take control and choose intentionally. If we tend to be cynical, then this is the message that becomes our mental model, our frame, through which we perceive ideas, communications, expe-riences—life. We then convert this into our reality. But if we choose to "reframe"—that is, delete the existing frame from our mind, and replace it with a different frame—we immedi-ately alter our perception, our physical, mental, and spiritual states, and our behavior and future actions. Being effective depends, very often, on reframing. Let me give you an example:

One of our health-care clients operates a very successful cardiology department. It has high volumes, significant rev-enues, and is one of the hospital's most profitable divisions. The old "frame" positioned this business as "the heart unit" which, to most of their team, meant providing appropriate surgical procedures for patients suffering from various heart ailments. And for many years, this was a successful philoso-phy. One day, they reframed their view of this business unit by proposing the creative idea of establishing a health club. They reasoned that a health club could be reframed as an extension of the heart unit. If patients followed good exercise and nutri-tion regimens, they would remain healthy—a goal shared by the heart unit. By integrating the two, they could expand their customer base—revenues would be generated either way—from paying customers of the health club, or from the cardiology department. If members of the health club failed to show up or practice the healthy lifestyles being taught at the health club, they might end up in another business unit owned by the same organization—the cardiology department. Eventually, their new health club grew to 20,000 members and was a runaway success, so that the cardiology department was now generating two separate income streams.

But this creative and inspired leadership team continued to reframe as they sought greater effectiveness. Because their health club was now so successful as an extension of their cardiology unit, they reasoned, perhaps there was an opportunity to franchise their system to other health-care facilities across the nation. So they manualized all their procedures, developed a start-up plan for new franchisees, which included club design, equipment purchasing, training, and marketing assistance, and created a third business—which also became part of the cardiology unit. All this was achieved by frequently reframing what they saw and reinterpreting this new data into more effective business practices.

Effective leaders reframe regularly, refusing to accept the status quo, always searching for a new way of seeing things—which others find inspiring—and therefore increase their effectiveness.

Collaborating for Effectiveness

Competitiveness is the default behavior in many organizations, and the principal doctrine in many leadership theories. But unlearning this limbic addiction and replacing it with collaboration—the honoring of other souls—is another example of the potential available to us to be more effective if we are prepared to unlearn "old-story" leadership ideas and replace them with "New-Story" leadership thinking.

Amazon.com develops sophisticated algorithms that enable it to recommend additional book or movie choices to customers based on their previous purchases. Many online retailers, including Netflix, the online movie rental company, do the same thing. In 2006, in an effort to improve its movie recommendation accuracy, the CEO of Netflix, Reed Hastings, established the Netflix Prize, a challenge to raise the accuracy of its recommendations by 10 percent. The prize: a cool $1 million. Forty thousand virtual teams from 186 countries signed up for the challenge.

Shortly after the contest began, some competing groups began to realize that going head to head with 40,000 other teams was leading to inferior solutions and that collaboration would be far more effective. Soon, they were sharing their information publicly on contest forums, and this raised the overall quality of everyone's proposals. Four different teams consisting of computer scientists, electrical engineers, and statisticians from Israel, Canada, the Unites States, and Austria (who would not meet until the awards ceremony) blended together to form team "BellKor" for the last push to win the prize by building a winning mathematical model.

Towards the end of the contest, Netflix organized a sort of quarter-finals process, in which the winners of these stages were required to make their methods available to all by publishing them on the Web site.

BellKor, the eventual winner, used some ingenious approaches— looking at *what* movies anonymous Netflix customers rated, instead of *how* they rated them; collecting data by genre or specific actor and mining that information for other clues, such as romance but no gun fights, or car chases but no violence.

Chris Volinsky, BellKor's team leader, said, "You need to think outside the box, and the only way to do that is find someone else's box. When we combined with other engineers, we found they approached the problem from a different perspective and we were able to use that to our advantage."

Though we tend to gravitate towards primal competitive

behavior, even *within* groups, and often choose to closely guard our proprietary information, more often, far greater effectiveness is achieved through sharing and collaboration. Towards the end of the contest, the BellKor team surpassed the original target of 10-percent improvement over the existing methods, but Netflix wanted to see if even more could be squeezed from the process, so all of the other contestants were invited to best the BellKor team's efforts in a final 30-day push. Nearly all the top-ranked teams merged into one to meet this challenge, but in the end, the BellKor team retained their lead and won the prize—but only by a whisker. The overall results were far more effective through sharing and collaboration than could otherwise have been achieved through more conventional competitive means.

The Circular Logic of the CASTLE Principles

All of the CASTLE Principles are interconnected—they are ONE. Like a giant emotional and spiritual hologram, every part is interconnected with every other part. Thus, one CASTLE Principle will be accomplished only through the engagement of the others. Understanding this is essential to effectiveness. We will be effective when we become the other five CASTLE Principles, and we become the other five CASTLE Principles by being effective. We call this *The Circular Logic of the CASTLE Principles*. Using the CASTLE Principle of Effectiveness as an example, the following summary describes this phenomenon:

- **Courage:** I cannot become effective unless I am first courageous. Because everything is initiated through courage, strengthening my effectiveness cannot happen until I have the courage to do what is necessary to be more effective. But the reverse is also true: I will be courageous when I choose to live in a fully effective way. The greater my courage, the greater my effectiveness. Courage and effectiveness are ONE.

- **Authenticity**: Inauthenticity is an inefficient use of energy. Authenticity is the transparent and effective use of all resources. When I am authentic, I build trust, and when I build trust, I create stronger relationships, which lead to greater effectiveness. I will be authentic when I see the power and effectiveness of authenticity.
- **Service**: To be effective, I must serve—effectiveness without a serving purpose is pointless. Unless you and I and the larger community are being served, service is not effective. Like engines, we deteriorate, or become ineffective, if we are not maintained (or serviced). I will serve others, or my organization, best when I first live in a fully effective way. And I will be most effective when I ensure that all my actions are serving others.
- **Truthfulness**: As Mark Twain said, "If you tell the truth, you don't have to remember anything." Telling the truth requires little effort; lying requires considerable negative energy. Lying is never effective, and when it is discovered, all advantage is lost. A lie always leads to betrayal, and betrayal always leads to a loss of trust. And effectiveness cannot be built without trust. I will be truthful when I practice the effectiveness of living truthfully.
- **Love**: If we can be as successful as we are by living as warriors, imagine what we could do by living in a loving and compassionate way. We would lose the toxicity, but none of the advantages, while gaining all of the benefits that loving, empathetic relationships can generate. Warriors destroy and dominate, creating fear and motivating with force. Leaders with a loving heart inspire others to greater effectiveness because everyone grows and thrives and no one dies. I will be fully loving when I commit to living in a fully effective way. And I will be most effective when I am a loving human being.

Growing Young Inspiring Leaders

I have often marveled at the frequency and persistence of dysfunctional behaviors among leadership teams, and this has caused me to reflect deeply on how we teach leadership and how this could be more effectively done in our educational system, because, it seems to me, if we were more effective at teaching values and inspiring leadership in our schools, the quality of the output might be greater. It seems a reasonable proposition that if we were to invest in significantly increasing the learning for students, enabling them to become inspiring leaders while at school, they might bring this awareness more broadly into their lives—including work. The ideal sequence of this learning process is to first teach students how to be inspiring—a topic that is absent from most levels of education—and later how to be an inspiring leader.

How would our educational systems become more effective, and how would students benefit, if the values inherent in the CASTLE Principles were incorporated into the culture of our schools and universities? North Gwinnett High School in the town of Suwanee near Atlanta, Georgia, is one of six schools in the North Gwinnett Cluster and part of the Gwinnett County Public Schools system—the 13th largest school district in the United States. Founded in 1958, the school has grown to become one of the leading schools in Gwinnett County and in the state of Georgia. With a teaching staff of almost 250, the school currently serves some 3,000 students.

In 2007, the school's then-principal, John Green, read about the CASTLE Principles in my book *ONE: The Art and Practice of Conscious Leadership* and realized that they would be a perfect complement to the leadership program he had initiated at North Gwinnett three years earlier based on the concepts of "lead yourself, lead your club or team, lead your school and community, lead your life." He felt that the CASTLE Principles fit perfectly with the school's vision that "*all* students are leaders, all students add value," and they could help to dispel the misperception that leadership is positional or hierarchical. Green shared this discovery with a colleague, Nancy Ward, who runs the Gwinnett County Student Leadership Team, and jointly they made the decision to introduce students to *ONE* and the CASTLE Principles. In a Fall retreat with the school's student leaders that year, Green based his presentation, which he titled "Leadership Mindset," on the CASTLE Principles.

Since then, the CASTLE philosophy has been absorbed into the culture and student leadership programs at North Gwinnett, alongside other leadership teachings of similar orientation. "The CASTLE Principles have served as a way to generate common language for our teacher-leaders and school leaders," says Green. "They represent a sort of integrative curriculum, pre-K through grade 12, because they can easily be understood by students at all levels, some even by five-year-olds. *Every kid* can do something to help another student, or to help someone else."

The concept of servant-leadership, and the notion of being other-focused, is deeply ingrained in the school's culture. The slogan "It's not all about me" serves as the cultural description of North Gwinnett's school community. And its transforming effects are immediately noticeable to others. In 2008, when Ed Shaddix assumed the school's leadership, taking over from John Green, who was promoted to area superintendent after ten years as principal, he realized quickly that this school was unlike any other he had ever been part of. It became obvious to him that his predecessor had built, as Shaddix says, "an unbelievable administrative team with high levels of trust and capability." At North Gwinnett, leadership was not just talked about—it was *lived*.

"Leadership is a huge component of the culture here," says Shaddix. "There is an expectation of behavior that the kids set for themselves, and that the community sets for them, that you don't find anywhere else. Everyone works in an atmosphere of mutual respect, and we hold the expectation that all students can learn at high levels. Our teachers believe it, our kids believe it, and our results prove it."

According to *Newsweek* magazine's "Top Public High Schools," North Gwinnett ranked number one in Gwinnett County and number 212 in America in 2008, up from 682 in 2004. The school's remarkable academic results support North Gwinnett's reputation as a model for other schools in the county and the state of Georgia, with 90 percent of graduating seniors attending post-secondary schools, and 46 percent of seniors receiving a total of more than $10 million in scholarships offered. In 2008, 65 percent of North Gwinnett's seniors had scored a "3 or better" on an advanced placement exam while in high school, which translates into two-thirds of the school's seniors having started college with at least one course credit earned in the advanced placement program. This figure is significantly above the state average of 25 percent.

Building on the strong foundation established by his predecessor, Ed Shaddix has implemented an effective tutoring system run by the school's students. In addition to helping each other—modeling the CASTLE Principle of Service—North Gwinnett's students serve as mentors to the younger students in the elementary and middle schools that feed into North Gwinnett.

Inspired by the same spirit of mentoring and servant-leadership, the administrative team at North Gwinnett offers assistance to other schools in the district and beyond. The school receives many visitors each year, often principals from other schools, who come to learn about its unique culture and academic environment. "We'd like for as many schools as possible to realize that once you adopt the philosophy of the CASTLE Principles, that all students can be leaders," says John Green," and that when you believe this, it can make a huge difference in what your students produce in terms of their work and how productive they become once they leave school and go on to college, and whatever it is they go on to do."

When asked how utilizing the CASTLE Principles has contributed to North Gwinnett's effectiveness, John Green shares a revealing insight: "Just as *Effectiveness* is the last letter in the

CASTLE acronym, so it also provides the validation for what you've done utilizing the other concepts. You can't help but be effective if you practice Courage, Authenticity, Service, Truthfulness, and Love. And so the Effectiveness becomes a validation component. I also see it as being multidimensional, where, for instance, the more love you can develop, the more effective you are. And while we need to recognize the unique value of each of the CASTLE Principles in terms of its contribution to overall effectiveness, it's important to recognize that they are all interconnected and working as one."

North Gwinnett is a model of Effectiveness and all six CASTLE Principles in action.

Effectiveness, Courage, and Commitment

As we have seen, we must first be inspired before we can be effective. Effectiveness is facilitated by Courage, because being effective requires that we invest more than a mediocre effort—more than merely what we can get away with, and that often requires courage. It requires extraordinary levels of commitment.

* * *

Many say that John Bachar was the greatest solo climber of all time. Most climbers use ropes, bolts, and pitons in their ascents, rappelling down the mountain using lines. John Bachar raised the bar for all climbers by eschewing all of these aids in a form known as free climbing or free soloing. His climbing style and courage were legendary, and he became a mythical and charismatic figure to many. He climbed shiny granite vertical walls like a spider, or, as he preferred to describe it, like a starfish. He moved very deliberately, almost in slow motion, placing a careful handgrip here, raising his leg parallel to his hip to a rim of rock there, hauling his body up with one arm, and repeating this balletic routine until he reached his destination. Unlike many mountaineers, he felt no urge to "conquer" the rock face, and "getting to the top" was not the point. What counted for John Bachar were the elegance, grace, and control of how he got there—as described in *The Essentials of Effectiveness* above.

Was he afraid of falling? By his own admission, he was terrified of heights, but he overcame these fears—thus becoming more effective—by practicing his moves first on boulders, from which he could fall five feet onto sand, and eventually working up to greater heights, until he could confidently climb up several hundred feet calmly with his palms open and relaxed, as if he were walking to the store. As he observed, we can walk on a line on the ground with no problem, but as soon as we place the same line on top of a building, we lose our confidence, and therefore our effectiveness. Confidence was a key word for John Bachar— and confidence is the product of courage, which leads to greater effectiveness. Did he dare look down? "Of course. It's beautiful up there." Besides, he added, "Just looking down isn't going to kill you." He knew the risks associated with free soloing were the price exacted by his passion for it.

Goethe wrote, "Knowing is not enough; we must apply. Willing is not enough; we must do." In order to maintain his courage, confidence, and effectiveness, John Bachar practiced and worked out two hours every day, perfecting his technique and honing the strength upon which his life would depend. At Camp IV in Yosemite, he built his own gym among the trees, in which he and his fellow pony-tailed idealists trained to be "masters of stone." They tied ropes to trees to practice tightrope-walking in order to enhance their balance and built hanging ladders that became known as Bachar ladders. He followed a strict nutritional regimen. His life was an evolution of courage, inspiration, commitment, and effectiveness: at 14, he was a weakling who could do only two pull-ups; at 16, when he made his first free ascent at Joshua Tree, he could do 27. By his mid-20s, he had mastered doing pull-ups with one arm, or with 140 lb of weights. At his peak, Bachar was able to perform a one-arm pull-up with 12.5 lb of weight in his other hand.

He would seem to grasp what appeared to be nothing—placing the special boots, made by his own company, on a mere blemish in the rock, a "smear," or a hairline crack, sometimes less than half an inch wide, suddenly freeing both arms from the rock to make a lunge to the next handhold. More than 50 feet up, one mistake could spell death, and he was often on faces of 200 feet or more.

Effectiveness also comes from focus and mental preparation. Bachar's training regimen was both mental and physical. The superior caliber of personal focus required to achieve exceptional levels of effectiveness is realized through learning how to simultaneously relax and concentrate. Many achieve this through the practice of meditation. Bachar's technique was to visualize nothing except the "little circle of rock" ahead of him, and emptying his mind of everything except the fluidity and perfection of his moves—in a way, his own form of meditation. If he required a surge of strength, he visualized throwing an electric switch to flood his muscles with power. He imagined his fingers to be steel hooks and himself as a dancer. His climbing was the opposite of reckless—he was a mathematician who was the son of a mathematician; at UCLA he majored in math prior to becoming a climber. Each mission up a polished granite tower was, for him, an act of analysis. Before each ascent, he would mentally divide each boulder problem into sections, and prepare his mental state according to three zones: zone 1, no harm if he fell; zone 2, hospital, but he'd survive; zone 3, death if he made a mistake.

It was better to backtrack, every move executed with elegance and grace in reverse, than to climb in a clumsy or clunky way. It was better, he said, to be a flawless failure than a mediocre success.

On July 5, 2009, John Bachar died while climbing alone at the Dike Wall near Mammoth Lakes in the eastern Sierra, near his home in California. He was 52, and until that fateful day, a bruised back had been his worst injury. He escaped many close calls, and each time, he believed, the rock had merely let him get away with it. The rock was his superior and, he felt, should remain as if it had never been climbed.

John Bachar's death did not make him a failure because the legacy he left was a string of firsts—ascents, challenges, and breakthroughs—in addition to his many protégés. Another legendary climber, John Long, observed, "There has never been anyone like John Bachar, and there never will be again." And Peter Croft, with whom Bachar, in 1986, made a one-mile vertical ascent in less than 14 hours, said, "Yosemite was *the* place, Bachar was *the* guy; that makes him more than just a climber."

Effectiveness is always personal. Effective groups and teams are only effective if their individual members are effective. That is why we concentrate on the practice of effectiveness at the individual level. Bachar was a classic example.

In fact, anything we choose to do well, such as being an inspiration for others or achieving mastery, requires, as John Bachar demonstrated, great commitment—and great commitment leads to effectiveness.

Effectiveness through Forgiveness

Eldon Taylor wrote, "When you forgive, you essentially undo the ability to blame. If there is nothing to blame, then you are in charge of your response to outside stimuli. There is less room for anger without blame. There is less to fear when you're empowered."

Effectiveness requires objectivity. If we have been betrayed or hurt by another, any resulting anger, feelings of revenge, sense of woundedness, spite, bruised ego, or shadow behavior will lower our effectiveness. These emotions cloud our judgment. Forgiveness not only removes the clutter from our perspective, it also transforms the other person by encouraging them to recreate a relationship, and relationships that are whole and inspiring are essential to effectiveness.

Forgiveness is not simply an act of altruism. It is a form of enlightened self-interest that leads to effectiveness. It is the removal of anger, which is an obstacle to effectiveness.

I have worked with many teams where individual members have been wronged by each other, sometimes long ago, and the grudge remains as an aggravation which is massaged daily. Ugly things are said about and done to each other, which significantly lowers the effectiveness of the team. After all, if we aspire to be a member of a high-performing team, how can this be achieved when those who are essential to each other's success are throwing boulders in front of each other?

What is required here are reconciliation and forgiveness. Without these, we cannot move on, or achieve something great, and the situation will remain uninspiring for both the victim and persecutor—even worse, it will drain the energy out of the entire team.

Forgiveness is a commitment to letting go of anger, resentment, and revenge. Resentment towards another is a negative-energy chord that connects you to them and keeps you bound until you decide to melt that destructive bond with forgiveness. The benefit of forgiveness is often greater for the person who forgives than for the one who is being forgiven—forgiveness sets a prisoner free, and often that prisoner is you. The role of the leader is to act as coach, mentor, arbitrator, broker, and healer with any team members who remain unwilling to forgive. No team can be effective—or whole—where forgiveness still waits to occur.

Forgiveness is the fragrance that the violet sheds on the heel that crushed it.

Mark Twain

PART THREE

THE TORCH

How Will You Pass It On?
What Will Your Legacy Be?
How Will You Share Your Wisdom with Others?

*T*he spark ignites the flame, and the flame sets fire to the *torch*. We convert the spark into a flame, using it to light the torch, which we pass to others. The torch is the legacy we create; it is the gift of mentoring, coaching, and supporting people's growth, so that their spark is awakened. The torch is paying it forward, teaching others, helping them to develop, and sharing the philosophy of inspiring leadership with them. And when we light another's torch, our own flame is never diminished. On the contrary, it burns even more brightly.

> *Sometimes our light goes out but it is blown again into a flame by an encounter with another human being. Each of us owes the deepest thanks to those who have rekindled this inner light.*
>
> Albert Schweitzer

Reflection Twelve:
Guiding Others to Greatness

We can choose to make the success of all humanity our personal business. We can choose to be audacious enough to take responsibility for the entire human family. We can choose to make our love for the World what our lives are really about. Each of us now has the opportunity, the privilege to make a difference in creating a World that works for all of us. It will require courage, audacity and heart. It is much more radical than a revolution, it is the beginning of a transformation in the quality of life on our planet. You have the power to fire a shot heard around the World. If not you, who? If not here, where? If not now, when?

Werner Erhard

How Fire Was Given to Humanity

Long ago, there were four brothers, Prometheus (Foresight), Epimetheus (Hindsight), Menoetius (Ruined Strength), and Atlas (Enduring). They were Titans and lived in the ancient Greek world.

Zeus, who ruled the world, did not want humans to prosper, and he was especially keen to ensure that they had no power over fire. Prometheus was saddened by the abject poverty and living conditions of humans, and he ached for the many who were barely surviving in caves and holes in the earth. Without fire, countless numbers of them perished from the cold. Others died from starvation or were savaged by wild beasts, and often even by each other. Their lives were wretched.

"I wish I could bring them fire," thought Prometheus, "for then they could warm themselves and cook their food, and in time they would be able to make tools and build homes."

He pleaded with Zeus to give humans fire, but Zeus was adamant, declaring that fire would give power to humans, and that they would use that power to threaten his own.

Prometheus was bitterly disappointed, but his heart was set on improving the human condition, and he resolved to never give up. He left Zeus and the luxurious and plentiful world of the Gods forever.

As he was walking along the edge of the seashore, he picked up a tall fennel reed and noticed that its hollow center was filled with a dry, soft pith. He reasoned that if this was lit, it could carry a flame for long time. He took the fennel stalk and began a long journey to the East where the sun dwelled.

"I will bring fire to humans even though the powerful Zeus forbids it," he said to himself.

His journey eventually brought him to the sun as dawn was emerging and the great glowing orb was rising from the earth to begin its daily journey across the sky. He reached toward the flames, and a spark caught the end of the long reed, igniting the dry pith, which began to burn very slowly. He turned his back to the sun and began his return to his own land, carrying with him the precious spark hidden deep in the pithy core of the reed.

When he arrived, he gathered some of the shivering, dejected people from their makeshift hovels, and from the spark in the fennel reed he created a flame and with it, he built a fire for them, teaching them how to heat themselves and build fires for others from the coals. Soon, many families were being warmed and comforted in their crude abodes, and happiness filled their hearts.

In time, these humans learned to cook and to change the savage and brutal practices of the past, turning instead to civil and pleasurable behaviors that brought joy.

Prometheus loved humanity, and after bringing fire to people, he continued to teach them a thousand things. He showed them how to collaborate with one another, how to build houses of natural materials, how to tame and domesticate wild animals, how to plow and sow and reap a harvest, and how to create security from the elements and the wild forms of nature. Then he showed them how to mine for minerals, to melt and shape them into tools, and he was joyful.

Prometheus loved the world. His gift was the enhancement of humanity. He lit a spark, carried a flame, and ignited the torches of others. We can call it Promethean leadership—the desire to create a legacy for the greater good. Inspiring leaders are Promethean leaders—leaders whose purpose in life is to serve the world and enhance it by igniting their spark and fueling and sharing their flame. Their commitment is to leave a legacy which will continue to light the way for others long after their work on this planet is completed.

Paying It Forward

The torch represents our role as teachers, guides, coaches, leaders, helpers, and supporters for others—Promethian leadership. As teachers lighting the flame for others with our torch, we will do well to remember William Arthur's advice: "The mediocre teacher tells. The good teacher explains. The superior teacher demonstrates. The great teacher inspires." Being inspired and inspiring carries with it the responsibility to share what we have learned—to pay it forward. In a letter accompanying a financial gift to a friend, Benjamin Franklin wrote, "I do not pretend to *give* such a Sum; I only *lend* it to you. When you shall return to your country with a good character, you cannot fail of getting into some business that will in time enable you to pay all your debts. In that case, when you meet with another honest man in similar distress, you must pay me by lending this Sum to him; enjoining him to discharge the debt by a like operation, when he shall be able, and shall meet with another opportunity. I hope it may thus go thro' many hands, before it meets with a Knave that will stop its Progress. This is a trick of mine for doing a deal of good with a little money."

Promethean leadership *pays it forward*, and paying it forward is about serving others.

By now, as you have worked your way through this book, you will be in the minority among human beings—an inspired and inspiring person—and you will have achieved awareness of two remarkable things: 1) The spark: *Why you are here*, and 2) The flame: *How you will inspire and lead*.

Now it is time for you to pass the torch, to share what you have learned with others, to continue to inspire, coach, lead, mentor, and guide them, so that they may do the same for others, and thus change the world. This is your legacy—the legacy of an inspiring leader.

Elegance and Simplicity in Design that Inspires

In passing the torch to others, we become teachers, coaches, mentors, guides, and leaders and models for others. Our lives are filled with methodologies and processes aimed at supporting the growth and development of others. There are two traditional and widely used ways in which effective leaders do this in organizations: 1) assessing the performance of others in order to help them to grow, and 2) coaching them towards the greatness that lies within us all. But our techniques in these two areas are often clumsy and ill-conceived.

One personal development approach used by many organizations is the almost universally reviled "performance appraisal" or "performance review." Stanford University professor Jeffrey Pfeifer recalls how, some years ago, the former head of Human Resources at SAS Institute was cheered when he led a celebration in which performance appraisals were fed into a bonfire—the Institute's research on performance appraisals having produced mixed results regarding their contribution to improving performance. Generally, neither the appraiser nor the appraisee are inspired by performance appraisals, so it is a wonder that we keep inflicting them on people. In fact, on nearly every occasion when I delivered a speech in which I suggested that we abandon performance appraisals altogether, I received a spontaneous standing ovation! For those for whom the process is a mechanical chore, there is a book called *Effective Phrases for Performance Appraisals: A Guide to Successful Evaluations,* which is a million-seller, now in its 12th edition, containing 3,500 useful phrases—a sort of CliffsNotes for managers. So, it seems that for some, the process of assessing the performance of others has been reduced to the exercise of identifying catchy phrases.

Mark Twain said, "All generalizations are false, including this one," so I am guarded about making a generalization here. I have worked with several organizations that have made great progress in humanizing their appraisal systems. But even in their cases, the performance-appraisal process still feels like an annual ritual approached resentfully by leaders and their followers—a frequently used but inaccurate metric. In this Reflection, we will attempt to reframe this process, so that all parties can find it inspiring. We could start by eliminating the uninspiring "old-story" terminology, "appraisal," and replace it with "attunement," defined in the dictionary as *being or bringing into harmony; a feeling of being "at one" with another being.* Assessment suggests a hierarchical relationship in which the appraiser is judging the appraisee. Attunement suggests an alignment of aspirations among parties, without judgment, leading to greater meaning and fulfillment—joy.

As we reviewed in Reflection Four, 5 Dynamics suggests that, to varying degrees, the energies drawn upon when we are learning fall into four categories: Explore, Excite, Examine, and Execute. And h*ow we learn is how we engage with the world.* Traditional performance appraisals engage the Excite and the

Examine energies and, by and large, bypass the other two. This is appropriate for those with learning styles favoring Excite or Examine energies, but what about the rest of the world? And what if you favor one, such as Explore, and are generally disinterested in Excite or one of the others? As you can see, the possible permutations are endless—there are four energies and four levels of intensity, all of which may provide another reason why so many people tend to be disengaged by this process. When we design methods of helping others to grow and learn, such as teaching, mentoring, coaching, and attunement—the torch—*all four* energies must be engaged if we want others to feel connected and inspired.

Executive, business, career, or life coaching is another approach to personal development—a process that seems to work better in tasks (such as sports, music, apprenticeships, art, etc.) than in the general applications to life. Although, worldwide, there are close to 100,000 registered coaches offering guidance to their clients, here, too, the data about the value of coaching is mixed. Business coaching is practiced in 70 countries, with the greatest concentration being in the United States, England, Japan, and Australia. The coaching industry has been growing by approximately 20 percent annually, with annual revenues approaching $2 billion. Seventy percent of coaches work mostly by telephone and e-mail, 70 percent are female, and the average age is between 40 and 55. There are over 65 coach training schools located worldwide, but even with the growth and success of the business and life coaching fields, neither has received the level of validation enjoyed by, for example, sports coaching. Establishing a coaching Return on Investment (ROI) continues to be elusive—none of my clients are able to quantify just how much hay the sun puts in the barn.

The causes of the mixed reviews of these two widely applied processes are different: the performance appraisal seems to suffer because of flaws in the approach and design of performance management programs and the review system, while coaching remains of questionable value because a breakthrough method-ology for personal development—at least in business and life coaching—has yet to be discovered. There is also a rush by the accrediting bodies to set unnecessary hurdles in the formaliza-tion process, overcomplicate the curriculum and the means of certification, and turn the coaching field into some sort of guild which excludes otherwise highly seasoned and qualified coaches and mentors.

As I have repeatedly emphasized, nearly everything that works well is simple, elegant, and graceful. When we complicate things, they become clunky and inefficient. Pseudo-sophistication in the design of processes, such as performance appraisals or coaching, has stalled the realization of their full potential. Often, the com-petitive arenas of the business schools or the consulting profes-sion generate such pseudo-sophistication at the expense of simplicity, elegance, and grace.

Inspiration versus Motivation

One other reason why coaching and performance management often fall short of their ambitions is the confusion we have cre-ated around the two words "motivation" and "inspiration."

Motivation is something we *do* to people. It comes from a combination of two sources: fear and material rewards or pun-ishments. Motivation is seldom about the other person, but more often about *me*. I need to meet my budget, so I am going to moti-vate all my sales team with incentives, so that they will achieve their sales goals, and if they do so, then I will meet *my targets*. When we are trying to motivate someone, we are typically seek-ing to alter or control behavior, raise performance standards, or exploit potential. When we come from this position, we are working principally on the personality of the person we are try-ing to motivate, and we are relying on shaming, bribing, reward-ing, threatening, or pressuring—all of which appeal to the primal instincts of fear. Often, too, we use the prospect of being in or out of favor as a motivational weapon. When we use fear in this way to coach or manage, the person being coached experiences anxiety and stress.

Most of our modern theory of marketing is based on motivation: "Buy my lotion or you will be ugly." Our religions are often based on fear: "Join my faith or you will go to hell." Politics run this way, too: "Vote for me or the other guy will raise your taxes." The way we run organizations often falls into this same pattern: "Do what I say, or we'll fire you." And, of course, performance management has long followed this path: "Reach these goals and we will reward you; miss them, and we will punish you." Motivation is extrinsic, relies on fear and material rewards or punishments, and is targeted at the ego or the personality. Motivation often gets things done—but at a price. And that price is often resentment, anger, lack of trust, and reprisal.

Inspiration is intrinsic. It does not come from fear, but from love. It is not about me—it is almost always exclusively about *you*. Great leaders and coaches want to inspire others to grow, to accomplish *their* objectives, to shine, to reach their potential and splendor. Any rewards for these inspiring coaches and leaders come from the joy they experience when helping others to reach *their own* goals or become larger as persons. If you think about the leaders, teachers, and coaches who made a difference in your life, they were all people who *loved* you. They would not have devoted the time and resources they did to you if they had not felt that way, and to this day, their loving legacy warms your heart. Inspiration is aimed at the soul of another, and is very often self-generated. As Galileo said, "You cannot teach a man anything. You can only help him discover it within himself." Indeed, this book describes how to ignite the spark of inspiration from within, and how that spark of inspiration can be fanned into a flame.

Whereas motivation is based on a need for each other, inspiration is based on love for each other. Motivation is based on fear, whereas inspiration is based on love. Motivation is ego- and personality-centered, while inspiration is soul-centered. Motivation is based on *me*, on serving my needs; inspiration is based on *you*, on serving *your* needs. Although we often use the words "motivation" and "inspiration" interchangeably, it can be seen from these arguments that they are nearly opposite in their meaning and intent. That we use them interchangeably also suggests that our understanding of the difference is weak, and because of this, we are not clear about when to use the one or the other. There is a place for motivation—if the building we are both in catches fire, I am going to motivate you to get out of there! Motivation is lighting a fire *under* someone; inspiration is lighting a fire *within* someone.

We have become experts at motivation. We now need to become just as effective at inspiring ourselves, inspiring others, and inspiring the world. Coaching and performance management—in fact, any means by which we enhance the spirit of another—will become more effective when we develop inspiring processes and focus on and grow our expertise in inspiring others.

Values-centered Leadership®: The Ultimate Coaching and Personal Development Model

Whatever practical accomplishment we seek in life requires the application of just three values: Mastery (doing something well), Chemistry (in a way that inspires others), and Delivery (so that we serve people and the world). The creation of great brands (such as Starbucks, Southwest Airlines, Disney, Apple) depends on these attributes. So does the personal success of people.

Think of a bicycle as a metaphor for an individual's or organization's life: imagine that the processes used by you or your team (or family, church, or organization—any group of humans) are arranged on the front and back wheels of your bicycle. Your power is derived from the back wheel and your direction from the front wheel. On the back wheel, we find the values that are the primary life skills that energize individuals, teams, and organizations. These are called Primary Values because they help us to kick-start personal development and growth, change attitudes, instill self-confidence, stretch and expand our horizons, and thus positively impact ourselves and others. In other systems, too, such as teams or organizations or countries, they are a prerequisite to success. We call this model *Values-centered Leadership*.[24]

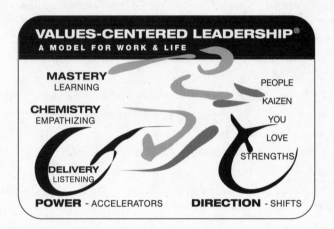

The Primary Values

To a greater or lesser extent, most of us know and practice these Primary Values every day. The difficult part is increasing our practice of them. The Primary Values on the back wheel are:

> **MASTERY:** Undertaking whatever you do to the highest standards of which you are capable
>
> **CHEMISTRY:** Relating so well with others that they actively seek to associate themselves with you
>
> **DELIVERY:** Identifying the needs of others and meeting them

---

[24] To learn more about the Values-centered Leadership® Model, and the Vector 360° Leadership Survey, please visit: www.secretan.com/vector

Note the words here—they have been chosen carefully. Mastery is about high standards—not Olympian, but the very best that you can accomplish *with some stretching*; Chemistry describes the quality of your relationship with others—as defined by *them*, not you; and Delivery is about service, on *their* terms.

Mastery

Mastery is the possession of the requisite skills, passion, and commitment to do whatever it takes to be the best in a particular task or specialty. An open mind—a learning mind—is a prerequisite. It requires a devotion to continuous personal and professional improvement, to setting standards for personal development, polishing one's skills, competencies, and practices, being an expert and respecting knowledge, wisdom, and learning. Mastery embodies a commitment to excellence in how we approach things. Walt Disney used to tell his employees, "Do what you do so well that others will come to see you do it again,"—that's Mastery. Our role as coaches, teachers, leaders, and mentors is the same: to do what we do so well that others will come to see us do it again—and to share that gift with others.

Mastery is a state of excellence. Ninety-eight percent of the journey to excellence is accomplished by many, but then the field narrows to those who are passionate about the last two percent. Catharine Pendrel, an Olympian cross-country mountain biker on the Canadian National Team, says, "I have that amazing race once, maybe twice a year…Afterward, I try to think back to what made everything come together. There are so many variables that this improvement, this two percent gain, could have come from any number of things. How did I travel for that event, what was my mental state, who did I travel and pre-ride with, how was my training, diet and sleep?…Be it luck, talent, hard work, or a combination that determines success, I'll continue my search for that two percent." This is the level of passion and commitment that is shared by those in pursuit of Mastery.

Chemistry

People with excellent Chemistry develop characteristics and attitudes that lead to the building of strong relationships. They have learned, and practice, Emotional Intelligence (EQ). They place a high value on harmonious interaction with others, taking the initiative to repair, maintain, and build friendships, and they seek to fathom the depths of their relationships, going beyond the usual superficialities. They understand the *feelings* of others and connect with them at that level. They know that interest in another is the most sincere form of respect. Truthfulness and promise-keeping are keystones of Chemistry and result in the establishment of emotional bonds with others built on trust. Those with excellent Chemistry enjoy the company of others as much as their own solitude, being team players as much as soloists.

Delivery

Delivery is honoring the sacredness of others, being respectful of their needs and having a passion for meeting them. It is the graceful pursuit of service, resulting in servant-leadership and the good of the other. This focus on the needs of others can sometimes be motivated by enlightened self-interest and altruism. Delivery honors meeting the needs of people over mere profit-making. Delivery is founded on "win-win" negotiations and relationships that treat customers, employees, suppliers—as well as friends, family, and strangers—as partners, allies, and collaborators, rather than adversaries, and it results in winning *with* them, not *over* them. Delivery is being concerned with doing the right thing more than doing things right.

The Accelerators

Though we would all like to be instantly, or easily, accomplished at Mastery, Chemistry, and Delivery, this is unrealistic. There are some practical steps that we need to take first. Mastery, for example, is accelerated by Learning—if we want to become more masterful in anything we aspire to do, we will need to learn something new. We already know what we need to know to achieve our *current* level of Mastery; if this were not so, our level of Mastery would be higher. In other words, our level of Mastery is dependent on our level of Learning, and we call Learning an Accelerator because it accelerates Mastery. Similarly, embodying great Chemistry with others is dependent on the Accelerator called Empathy, and achieving higher standards of Delivery depends on greater Listening. The three Primary Values of Mastery, Chemistry, and Delivery, therefore, depend on the three Accelerators of Learning, Empathizing, and Listening, respectively.

Learning. If Mastery is chopping wood, then Learning is sharpening the ax. As indicated in Reflection Six, the dictionary defines leading as "showing the way to" and teaching as "showing how to." Therefore, leading is teaching and teachers show learners how to learn. A teacher/leader is able to be more effective with a learner than with a knower—and often, our egos trick us into becoming knowers instead of learners. Eric Hoffer has written, "In times of change the learners will inherit the earth while the knowers will find themselves beautifully equipped to deal with a world that no longer exists." The unevolved ego frequently sabotages learning. The knower gets stuck; the learner is open and growing.

In 1846, a young Austrian-Hungarian doctor named Igaz Semmelweis investigated a notorious maternity ward in which nearly all of the inpatients contracted a fatal case of childbed fever. In the course of his investigations, he noticed that women who came into the ward after giving birth seldom became ill.

When a professor who cut his finger in the middle of an autopsy in that same hospital died of symptoms identical to those of these unfortunate mothers, Semmelweis reasoned that the students doing the autopsies were somehow transferring the fever to the women in the maternity ward.

Semmelweis began requiring that his students disinfect their hands before delivering babies, and the number of childbed fever cases dropped. Here is where "change" became difficult.

Semmelweis was labeled insane by his colleagues for having the audacity to suggest that they should wash their hands between deliveries, and they fired him. He tried to continue his research, but was ostracized by the medical community. His own mental health eventually deteriorated, leading to his death in an insane asylum.

One final event leading to the general acceptance of germs occurred in 1860. A famed doctor was scheduled to speak at a conference at which he intended to thoroughly denounce Semmelweis's ideas. Just as he began his speech, he was interrupted by a man who proceeded to tell the audience that he had discovered the bacterium responsible for childbed fever. That man was Louis Pasteur, and the rest is history.

Lack of proper hand washing continues to be the primary reason why MRSA and other superbugs are spread in hospitals today. Every year, 1.7 million patients in the United States develop infections while in hospital and 99,000 of them die, adding $30 billion to the nation's health-care bill. Despite overwhelming research and evidence supporting the importance of hand washing in disease control, some physicians and clinicians still do not consider it essential to wash their hands.

As this example shows, change is hard, as we all know, and even when we are faced with indisputable evidence that should direct our actions, we still sometimes find "the old ways" easier—the knowers eclipse the learners.

For learners, greater Mastery is achieved through the natural flow of learning from masters, coaches, mentors, and leaders—in person or through their teachings. Mastery is never perfect, just as there is no perfect knowledge or wisdom. Knowledge and wisdom are always incomplete, and so continuous learning—that is, lifelong learning—is essential if continuous Mastery is to flourish in all areas of our work and personal lives. Notice that the Accelerator for Mastery is Learning, not training; training is for dogs, Learning is an attitude.

In tough times—in fact, in any times—relevance, which is derived from Mastery and Learning, is essential. Survival as a species, as an organization, as a team, or as an individual depends on relevance. When we are relevant, we inspire; when we are irrelevant, we discourage and dissuade. Relevance, then, is essential to survival, at any level. We simply have to be brilliant and masterful at whatever we do. When I walk into a coffee shop and find it empty, it is easy to see why: the place is a mess; the staff don't care, and they aren't learning; the stock is low; and it is not enticing or inspiring for me. When I walk into another coffee shop and see lines trailing out of the door, the reason is just as simple: they do what they do as well, and often much better, than anyone else. People care and brighten your day. The other day while I was paying for my coffee in a Starbucks store, one of the baristas offered me a free sample of hot vanilla cider and a mushroom turnover. This is simple and brilliant—a demonstration of Mastery and constant Learning and improvement that leads to better service and an inspiring experience. Most importantly, it is relevant to *me*. Those who are masters at what they do, and are relevant themselves, are supporting the relevance of their organization, and therefore dramatically lower their own risk of being laid off in tough times.

Things change. The environment changes. People change. Tastes change. Technology and innovation change. The game changes. We have to keep up. If we aren't relevant, we become obsolete—whether we are a company or an individual. Even in tough times, I'll find the resources to buy what you offer if it is highly relevant to who I am and what I do.

When we focus on Mastery and Learning, and therefore relevance, we get better, and when we are better, we are valued.

Empathy. Empathizing is the second Accelerator. To be a friend (Chemistry), we must walk in the moccasins of others, because to relate with them well, we must first understand them. This is often best achieved by imagining their feelings, emotions, and sensitivities; by thinking how we would *feel* if we were in their situation and then trying to behave as we would want them to. People will forget what you said, or what you did, but they will never forget how you made them feel. And as Patsy Cline said, "If you can't do it with feeling, don't." So, our goal is to be in a continuous state of Empathy, behaving in a way that would make each of us the kinds of people with whom we would want to be friends if our roles were reversed. This leads to great Chemistry.

Paul Levy is the CEO of Beth Israel Deaconess Medical Center in Boston. As the 2009 recession began to savage his organization, he was faced with some grim choices—revenues and costs were clearly out of balance. "Old-story" leaders—the knowers—in other organizations were doing what they had always done in these situations: they fired employees. But Paul Levy is a Higher Ground Leader.

Prior to making his decisions, Paul Levy spent several days visiting the people most likely to be affected by staff cutbacks. He visited the nurses' stations and noticed the staff navigating the halls with the patients in their wheelchairs. He watched them engaging, chatting, and joking with the patients, making them feel comfortable and at ease. He watched the food staff delivering meals and being ambassadors for the hospital, chatting with patients and their families. They were, he thought, practicing medicine. As he observed these committed employees, changing beds, polishing floors, cleaning toilets, removing trash, he realized that many were immigrants, some had second jobs, and that their work was financially and professionally essential to them.

As he approached the all-staff meeting at the hospital's Sherman Auditorium to announce his plans, he saw these same people—anxious, fearful, expecting bad news—clinicians, clerical staff, therapists, nurses, all vital members of an 8,000-strong team that ensured the smooth running of a great hospital.

He took a breath as he began. "I want to run an idea by you that I think is important, and I'd like to get your reaction to it. I'd like to do what we can to protect the lower-wage earners— the transporters, the housekeepers, the food service people. A lot of these people work really hard, and I don't want to put an additional burden on them."

Pausing, he continued, "Now, if we protect these workers, it means the rest of us will have to make a bigger sacrifice. It means that others will have to give up more of their salary or benefits."

Deafening sounds of grateful and sustained applause immediately filled the Sherman Auditorium. Paul Levy was flooded with emotion. He choked up and paused. Gathering his emotions, he explained to all these essential team members that he wanted to hear from them with their ideas.

E-mails began pouring in to Paul Levy's office—about 100 per hour. Most of them said that they wanted to contribute to Beth Israel and would do what it took to ensure that no one lost their job. One nurse said her team voted unanimously to forgo a three-percent raise. An employee in the finance department, still stinging from being laid off from his previous position at a hospital in Rhode Island, proposed a four-day week. A respiratory therapist suggested eliminating bonuses. Others volunteered to forgo vacation time and sick leave.

Paul Levy used Empathy to transform fear into inspiration. His example puts a lie to the idea that we cannot say difficult things or convey bad news in ways that are inspiring. *Every* communication can be an inspiring one. Empathy builds Chemistry and leads to inspiration, which, in turn, raises passion and performance. The "old-story" approach inflicts pain; the "New-Story" way inspires.

Listening. Listening is the third Accelerator. We cannot meet the needs of others (Delivery) if we do not pause to hear what those needs are. Listening is not "not talking." To truly listen, we must shut down our "mental chatter" and genuinely, and nonjudgmentally, listen to each other. Then, and only then, can we hear each other's needs, and only then will we be in a position to take the appropriate actions to meet them. Of all human skills, Listening is perhaps the most difficult. In one exercise that I sometimes use in my seminars, participants are divided into groups, with those in one group being required not to talk, but to only listen to those in the other group. When the Listening is complete, and following some moments of silence, they may commence talking again. They always tell me how exhausting they find a full day of intentional Listening. This is because it is an unfamiliar activity for them—for most of us. We spend much of the time that others are talking rehearsing our next great speech which we will deliver as soon as they are finished—sometimes even before! The fact that Listening is such hard work probably explains why we do so little of it—there is a reason why we have one mouth and two ears! We are experiencing a growing social ailment—a sense that we are not being heard. It starts in our youth, with our parents and friends, and continues throughout our lives. Not being listened to—or heard—is at the root of most arguments, failed relationships and marriages, politicians who disappoint, teams and leaders that fail, revolutions, strikes, resignations, and corporate collapse. Unconditional and totally attentive Listening is a beautiful gift to the soul of another. Arguments and conflicts are caused when people stop listening to each other, focusing instead on convincing others of their points of view, explaining them to each other in as many different ways as possible until they "win." Conversely, conflicts are always resolved as soon as both parties agree only to ask questions, cease making assertions, and *listen.*

The Vector as a Coaching and Personal Development Tool

A *vector* is defined as *a quantity, such as velocity, completely specified by a magnitude and a direction.* The Vector in Values-centered Leadership is a tool that measures the relationship between the Primary Values and the Accelerators.

Most coaching or appraisal or personal and leadership development tools take snapshots of things as they are at the moment of assessment. They do not represent a living, dynamic picture, but a static one in which the conditions are freeze-framed. The absence of any accurate estimate of the likely outcomes that will be generated by the current status weakens the value of such tools. The purpose of the Vector is to add all three dimensions: a review of the past, a picture of the present, and a forecast of the future.

Here is how it works: In order for a Primary Value to grow, the magnitude of the Accelerator must be *greater* than the magnitude of the Primary Value. This is calculated by deducting the magnitude of the Primary Value from the magnitude of the Accelerator. Thus a magnitude of 7 for Mastery and 8 for Learning would result in a *positive* Vector of 1. Conversely, a magnitude of 8 for Mastery and 7 for Learning would result in a *negative* Vector of 1. In this way, we are able to predict the likely *velocity, magnitude, and direction* of the expected change—the Vector, or the *forward delta.*

THE VECTOR				
THE PRIMARY VALUES	(A) SCORE 0-10	THE ACCELERATORS	(B) SCORE 0-10	VECTOR (B) - (A)
MASTERY Undertaking whatever you do to the highest standards of which you are capable		**LEARNING** Seeking and practicing knowledge and wisdom		
CHEMISTRY Relating so well with others that they actively seek to associate themselves with you		**EMPATHIZING** Considering the thoughts, feelings, and perspectives of others		
DELIVERY Identifying the needs of others and meeting them		**LISTENING** Hearing and understanding the communications of others		

©The Secretan Center Inc.
e-mail info@secretan.com
Tel 519-927-5213   www.secretan.com

For any of the Primary Values to grow, there must exist a *positive* Vector. Thus a negative Vector suggests a future decline of that specific Primary Value, and a positive Vector suggests a future growth in that Primary Value. When we use these indicators in an inspiring way—a *Vector Dialogue*—we have at our disposal a new methodology for coaching and performance management.

All successful relationships and human actions depend on the routine practice of the back-wheel values—the combination of the Primary Values and the Accelerators. Friendships are built on them; high performance depends on them; they define customer service and employee satisfaction; they lead to effective meetings and negotiations; marriages grow stronger through their daily use. Anywhere and anything that requires a connection with people will get stronger through the maintenance of a positive Vector.

As we pass the torch to others, helping them to grow, to become more effective, and to live fulfilling and meaningful lives, the Vector becomes an invaluable tool. It is nonjudgmental, other-centered, and inspiring instead of coercive. It is calibrated against the possibilities envisioned by the other person—not the coach, mentor, or leader. It is a collaborative synthesis—of the hopes of one, and the guidance of the other—an alignment, or attunement, of aspirations.

The Vector Dialogue is contrarian because it departs from received wisdom and breaks most of the conventional rules about performance standards and coaching. Some of its unique attributes are:

1. It is a partnership conversation, not a hierarchical procedure.
2. It relies exclusively on asking questions, not on providing answers.
3. It is a dialogue between two souls, more than between two personalities.
4. It is not demanding, intimidating, or assertive, but compassionate, supportive, and inspiring.

5. It relies more on inspiration than motivation.
6. It is not fear-based, but is founded on a loving exchange.
7. There is no possibility of failure; any aspiration that serves, leads to personal growth, and makes the world better, is a useful destination (see page 26).
8. It is uniquely personal, not standardized.
9. It does not need to conform to any predetermined or universal standards, larger corporate systems, or goals.
10. It does not need to be work-related; any service or growth that enhances people and the world is a valid aspiration (see page 26).
11. The organizational goal is not the necessary condition; the only relevant criterion is personal growth—if every person grows, teams and organizations grow, and that energy can be directed into higher organizational performance.
12. The goal of both parties is to have their respective aspirations met to the satisfaction of each—attunement.
13. Complexity represents sand in the gears; the Vector is a fundamentally simple process.

When reviewing performance, coaching others, mentoring, or leading, we often focus on the snapshot taken—the performance achieved to date, or the personal accomplishments at the time. From this freeze-frame perspective, there is only a minimal view of *what the future holds*. But inspiring mentors[25] and leaders are deeply interested in passing the torch, in the *progress* of people—how they will grow and flourish in the future. The Vector is an indispensable measure of *likely* change. Assessing Mastery, for example, one might enjoy a magnitude of 10 and be considered exemplary in that domain. If all we choose to see is the current value and quality of Mastery, we will have no sense of what the future holds. But if we go further, not only noting the magnitude

---

[25] In Greek mythology, Mentor was the faithful and wise friend of Odysseus, and teacher and trusted guide to his son Telemachus.

of Mastery being 10, but *also* observing that the magnitude for Learning (the Accelerator for Mastery) is 8, then we notice that this produces a negative Vector of 2, and even though the level of 10 for Mastery is outstanding, it may raise the question of whether there is insufficient power in Learning to maintain that level. In other words, while the present may appear brilliant, the Vector can inform us that, in this case, the sustainability of this level is doubtful without a positive change in the magnitude of the Accelerator. Conversely, a magnitude of 8 for Mastery, and 10 for Learning, yields a positive Vector of 2, which might indicate a potential rise in the future level of Mastery—a delta of +2. In this case, where a level of 8 for Mastery might have drawn criticism from an "old-story" manager, being able to identify a level of 10 for Learning—a Vector of +2—suggests that this has already been identified and solutions are being sought.

In this way, conversations that center on developmental questions (What would you like your Mastery to be? Do you wish to grow? Are you happy with your current level of Mastery? Do you wish to influence the magnitude of your Vector?) offer opportunities for coaching, leadership development, and personal growth. They also serve to initiate a dialogue that is nurturing and inspiring and nonjudgmental.

The Shifts

The values on the back wheel provide Power to our lives and our organizations, as well as Acceleration. But our motives can be flawed unless they are tempered by the *shifts* on the front wheel that provide our Direction. While most of us are familiar, to a greater or lesser degree, with the back-wheel values, we simply need to increase our practice of them. This cannot be said of the front-wheel shifts; they are qualitatively different. Most of us are not committed practitioners of the shifts on the front wheel—in fact, we need to *shift* from an "old-story leadership" approach to a "New-Story leadership" one, and this is why we call the front-wheel values "shifts." They are:

- A *shift* from me to YOU: focusing more on the needs of others than our own
- A *shift* from things to PEOPLE: valuing people more than material things
- A shift from breakthrough to KAIZEN: celebrating the importance of doing things better just as much as doing them differently
- A *shift* from weaknesses to STRENGTHS: building on our strengths just as often as searching for and criticizing weaknesses
- A *shift* from competition and fear to LOVE: inspiring and motivating each other with love instead of fear and competition

From me to you. We are emerging from one of the most self-absorbed eras in human history. The personality-driven way is dangerously egocentric and counter-productive. Values-centered Leadership is other-centered and seeks collaborative win-win combinations. It assumes that when we help others to grow, find fulfillment, and experience joy, we all win. It recognizes that a proposition that is good for me but bad for you is, in the end, bad for both of us. It pursues a concept of oneness, honoring the sacredness of others and favoring a holistic, systems approach in which the members of any team are keenly aware of their impact on all other parts of the system. The Higher Ground Leader thinks in even larger terms, because for them, *you* includes *everything* else—people, the environment, and the universe. To the Higher Ground Leader, the shift from me to *you* assumes that a customer is more than a walking credit card, and an employee more than a means of production, and a river more than a discharge site—because they are all *you*.

We are all in service, meeting the needs of employees, customers, suppliers, communities, and our world, and if we do so brilliantly, all the time, we will be rewarded with advocates—dedicated and loyal employees who no longer dread work, but celebrate its rewards and have fun doing it; a growing crowd of customers who become our word-of-mouth marketers; and a support team of suppliers who love doing business with us and partner with us for success. More importantly, a shift from me to you offers a much-needed balance to the preoccupations flowing from our personalities, by shifting our focus from an exclusive emphasis on metrics, politics, and power to honoring the sacredness of others, serving them and our planet.

From things to people. The Bernies—Madoff and Ebbers—established the low point of questing for things at the expense of people. The genius of Western management has been our unsurpassed ability to acquire, measure, analyze, and count materiality—things. But in revering analysis and acquisition, we have forgotten that organizations are the sums of people, not of things. In fact, they are even more than that—they are the sums of the human spirits within them. It is the soul that inspires and becomes inspired, not things. Now, we must return to our true reason for existing by shifting away from our unhealthy addiction to things to a renewed commitment to people. The "things" approach only obeys hierarchy, order, politics, metrics, procedures, policies, manuals, formal systems, and structure. The "people" approach seeks to honor the heart, respect the soul, and lift the spirits of all—*while being effective at the same time.*

From breakthrough to kaizen. The favorite heroes of management gurus are breakthrough specialists: great inventors, entrepreneurs, promoters, and marketers. They are the hares who turn their innovative breakthroughs into personal fortunes, but we need to celebrate tortoises, too—and just as passionately. As Aesop said, "Slow and steady wins the race." There are two ways to grow: by innovation and breakthrough (finding a different way) and kaizen (finding a better way).

The capacity to do the same thing a little bit better every day may not look like a spectacular achievement in the short run, but it is in the long run. The Japanese call this kaizen (*kai:* better, and *zen:* good) or "continuous improvement in personal life, home life, social life, and work life, involving everyone." But it is not simply a Japanese idea; it is an intelligent idea. It is an attitude that honors the act of micro-excellence achieved through daily personal Mastery and Learning.

Many companies use *kaizen* techniques to achieve unheard-of improvements in quality and input. The Sony plant in Terre Haute, Indiana, that manufactures compact discs for Sony video games is an example. In 2009, it manufactured 2,715 products per person-hour, whereas just the previous year, 13 operators were required to manufacture 369 products in the same time. It produces 27 million disks each month, and these efficiencies have been achieved without any layoffs. But continuous improvement (*kaizen*) has wider application than the workplace: it is just as important in our personal lives—in our relationships, personal growth, politics, education, health and wellness, and spiritual development. To continuously improve in every aspect of our lives is to continually grow, and this is how we remain relevant and vital.

From weaknesses to strengths. Researchers claim that during an average business meeting, each idea introduced is met with nine criticisms. According to Marilyn L. Kourilsky, former dean for teacher education at UCLA's Graduate School of Education, 97 percent of kindergarten children in the United States think creatively, only 3 percent form their thoughts in a conforming, structured manner. By the time they complete high school, the balance has begun to shift—46 percent think creatively, while a more rigid, structured style is preferred by 54 percent. The process of losing our individuality, passion, and creativity is completed in the workplace: by the time we are 30, a mere 3 percent enjoy the freedom of practicing holistic, original thought processes, while 97 percent of us subject all our thinking to a structure which screens for orthodoxy, social correctness, and conflict avoidance—a process for which Irving Janis coined the term "groupthink."[26] In other words, we begin our lives with a learning, open, and curious attitude, but eventually we fall under a spell of creative and spiritual impotence—the journey from learners to knowers. We do not start out thinking like "old-story" leaders—it is something that we acquire. By criticizing, judging, and finding fault with the ideas of others, we suck the self-esteem from the souls of individuals and therefore organizations. We pounce on our flaws, missed targets, delayed projects, or budget overruns, and fail to celebrate our strengths or study and perfect our successes. By mistakenly placing our faith in the Aristotelian notion that by attacking ideas, we will strengthen them, we have perfected the skills of the ego and abandoned the gifts of the soul. But imagine if every person and every organization devoted as much passion and time to building on their strengths, to celebrating what is working *more* than criticizing and judging what is not—our souls would begin healing until we became extraordinary and inspired.

Psychologist James Loehr, who has helped to train, among others, tennis great Martina Navratilova, has studied what the best tennis players do when they take a 20-second break between points during a match. Loehr discovered that mediocre players use that time to react to the previous point—scolding themselves after a missed point, for example. The best players, Loehr found,

---

[26] *Groupthink: Psychological Studies of Policy Decisions and Fiascoes*, Janis, Irving Lester; Houghton Mifflin; 2nd edition (1983)

spend the time preparing for the next point, relaxing, energizing themselves, planning their strategy, and tuning their minds.

From Competition, Hostility, and Fear to Love. In Reflection Eight, we discussed how the "old story" of leadership makes marketing a warrior practice. Businesses dedicate enormous amounts of people-power, time, and energy to the objective of defeating opponents, crushing competitors, and creating losers. Modern leadership language is laced with metaphors of war and aggression, and team members often feel like faux-warriors on a quest to conquer competitors in the battle for market share. Of course, none of this is inspiring. It is frightening. While the social self may become engaged with these metaphors, the essential self recoils. War is anathema to the soul. Life is more than an endless competition in which we are all gladiators at some level, seeking to vanquish our opponents, who, the social self conveniently forgets, are sitting at the next desk, or riding home with us on the train.

Life is not a battleground—it's a playground. War or the fear of losing does not inspire people. We would rather have chocolate cake to dream for than die for. Extraordinary accomplishments or performances are inspired and romanced from people, not beaten out of them. If we love what we do (Mastery), love the people with whom we do it (Chemistry), and love the reason for doing it (Delivery), would we still call it work? People are inspired to do what they do well by the *love* they feel for what they do (Mastery), the people they do it with (Chemistry), and their reasons for doing it (Delivery).

The front-wheel shifts, then, are modifiers for the Primary Values and Accelerators on the back wheel. For example, we might rate a "10" in Mastery as the finest con artist in the world, but if we only score a "1" in the shift "from me to you," the *quality* of the Mastery is devalued and questionable.

Values-centered Leadership as a Base Operating System

The Values-centered Leadership model is as effective in work-related situations as it is in personal ones. For example, in the work-related context, the model has been used to develop business plans, customer feedback programs, service and quality standards, compensation plans, performance assessments, consensus building, leadership feedback, and project management plans. It can be seen that any of these can be divided into these three components:

1. **Mastery:** What must we do well in order to accomplish this objective? What must we **Learn** to achieve the necessary Mastery?
2. **Chemistry:** To achieve our goals, who will be on this team? How will we build relationships and inspire each other? With whom should we **Empathize**?
3. **Delivery:** Whom are we serving? How will we know that we have met their needs? To whom and how will we **Listen**?

These questions, and others like them, serve to fill in the blanks for anything that we wish to build, grow, or develop. They serve a similarly useful role if we wish to build, grow, or develop people. It is a coaching, mentoring, and leadership model, and it is a life-model, not just a work-model, transferable to any situation and usable in any context. It has been effectively used in educational settings (teacher/student effectiveness), the home (parent/child communications), the political arena (elected official/constituent feedback), therapy (counselor/patient discussion), and among friends. It is an integrative, holistic process that works well in any condition where individuals or groups must interact with each other in order to be effective and fulfilled. It incorporates a standard language—a lingua franca—which can be used as a template in any situation. Though Mastery, for example, will mean something different for an air traffic controller than it will for a musician, we still intuitively understand, generally speaking, what Mastery means and how it might apply to those differing activities. With practice, you will find that the language and the values become second nature for you and a vital tool for renewing your soul.[27]

> *In every art beginners must start with models of those who have practiced the same art before them. And it is not only a matter of looking at the drawings, paintings, musical compositions, and poems that have been and are being created; it is a matter of being drawn into the individual work of art, of realizing that it has been made by a real human being, and trying to discover the secret of its creation.*
>
> Ruth Whitman

---

[27] See, for example, the chapter of my book *Reclaiming Higher Ground: Creating Organizations That Inspire the Soul* (The Secretan Center Inc., 2003) entitled "Blithe Spirit," in which I have described how to use the Values-centered Leadership model to define and measure personal goals.

POSTSCRIPT

The purpose of our work is more than just material—it is also spiritual. Inspired work is the result of inspired leadership—and this comes from the heart. And as Ram Dass said, "When I look at the human heart, that link, that doorway, I see an institution that makes the Pentagon look like kids' toys." We don't change the world merely by going to work in the morning just to manufacture widgets or produce reports. We change the world by engaging our heart, that most amazing, complex, and powerful instrument of human potential, and we do that by going to work to live our Destiny, Character, and Calling—our Why-Be-Do—to be of service to each other, to realize a dream, and to contribute to the healing and recovery of the planet. Each of us has chosen a different means of working, different skills, different organizations, products, and services, but we can all unite in a shared goal: to celebrate and honor each other and make our planet more peaceful, beautiful, and loving.

When Phil Jackson, the coach of the NBA champion teams the Chicago Bulls and the Los Angeles Lakers, won his tenth NBA championship in 2009, he became arguably the greatest coach in basketball's history. Writing about that unique moment, Adrian Wojnarowski observed, "For everyone who says they would've won with Michael Jordan and Shaquille O'Neal and Kobe Bryant, understand this: There are few coaches alive who could've commanded the respect of those players for all those years, all those championships. Maybe just one, just Jackson."

Wojnarowski describes Jackson this way: "As much as anyone, he understands that the genius of coaching isn't in the X's and O's but the humanity of it all. 'He coaches unity and chemistry and togetherness,' Bryant said. He coaches the human condition. All those coaches who say, well, give me Kobe Bryant, just understand: He [Kobe Bryant] would've eaten most of them alive."

We have danced together for more than 200 pages, covering our ideas of what Kobe Bryant referred to as "unity, chemistry, and togetherness" to forge a better appreciation for leadership, by becoming inspired and inspiring. We have shown that to become inspired and therefore inspiring, we must find a way to light our spark. We do this by defining our Destiny, Character, and Calling—our *Why-Be-Do*—having a Dream, identifying our energies and learning styles, and strengthening our relationship-building skills through the use of 5 Dynamics. Igniting the spark means healing the past, living the present, and dreaming the future.

Then we fan the spark into a flame by practicing the CASTLE Principles: Courage, Authenticity, Service, Truthfulness, Love, and Effectiveness. The flame is the brightness of how we live our lives, rather than how we talk or think about it. The flame is how we shine light upon the world and make it a better place than we found it.

Letting Go of Old Ideas

Two monks who were traveling together decided to rest by a river.

Soon, a young woman arrived, and wary of the current, she asked if they would be kind enough to carry her across.

One of the monks hesitated, but the other quickly picked her up onto his shoulders, transported her across the water, and gently lowered her onto the ground on the other side of the river. She thanked him for his kindness and departed.

As the monks continued on their way, the one was brooding and thoughtful. Unable to contain himself any further, he spoke out. "Brother, our spiritual training teaches us to avoid any contact with women, but you picked that one up on your shoulders and carried her!"

"Brother," the second monk replied, "I set her down on the other side, while you are still carrying her."

Letting go of old ideas is perhaps the most difficult obstacle to change and becoming inspired and inspiring.

It is not our words that make our flame bright so much as our deeds. As Albert Schweitzer said, "Example is not the main thing in influencing others. It is the *only* thing." [italics mine]

We pass the torch to others by coaching, mentoring, leading, and serving them, and we measure our progress as guides, and the progress of those who are new to carrying their own torch, through the Values-centered Leadership model. And we do so by sharing what we have and what we have learned. It is how we grow—both the one with the flame, and the one with the torch. George Bernard Shaw described it this way, "If you have an apple and I have an apple and we exchange these apples, then you and I will still each have one apple. But if you have an idea and I have an idea and we exchange these ideas, then each of us will have two ideas." Thus the flame is passed to the torch.

I hope you will find that these parts integrate comfortably into a seamless whole, enabling us to see the oneness in everything we do, honor the sacredness of others, and inspire the world. This is how we become inspired people and inspiring leaders.

> *The situation of the soul in contemplation is something like the situation of Adam and Eve in paradise. Everything is yours, but on one infinitely important condition: that it is all given. There is nothing that you can claim, nothing that you can demand, nothing that you can take. And as soon as you try to take something as if it were your own—you lose your Eden.*
>
> Thomas Merton

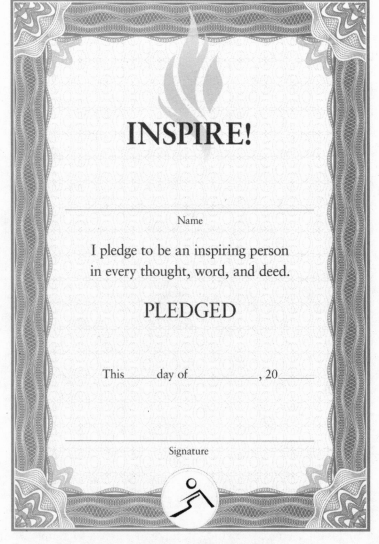

INSPIRE!

_____
Name

I pledge to be an inspiring person
in every thought, word, and deed.

PLEDGED

This_____day of_____, 20_____

_____
Signature

*Please sign the **Inspire Pledge** at*
www.secretan.com/inspirepledge

Becoming a Torchbearer

The Spark, the Flame, and the Torch is a manifesto for the Secretan Center's ONE Dream™ of "Changing the world by creating inspiring organizations." If you would like to join the growing community of people who wish to *Inspire Self, Inspire Others, and Inspire the World*, there are several avenues open to you.

Contact Us at These Coordinates:

The Secretan Center Inc.
Caledon, Ontario
Canada

Phone: 519-927-5213
Fax: 519-927-3909
E-mail **info@secretan.com**
Web: **www.secretan.com**

Web Site:

Please visit our main Web site at **www.secretan.com** and the Web site for *The Spark, the Flame, and the Torch* at **www.secretan.com/torch**. There, you will find many helpful ideas, free downloads, links to materials to support you in further study of the ideas presented in this book, and guidelines for setting up a book discussion group for *The Spark, the Flame, and the Torch*.

Please remember to sign the Inspire Pledge at
www.secretan.com/inspirepledge

**Keynotes, Workshops, Retreats,
Consulting, and Coaching**
To book Lance Secretan to address your conference,
group, or organization, please go to this Web address:

www.secretan.com/meetingplanners

If you would like any of the Secretan Center faculty
or coaches to work with you, please contact us at
info@secretan.com.

Learning More:
For resources you can use to bring *The Spark, the Flame,
and the Torch* more fully into your life or your organization, please visit our Web site. There are teachers and
coaches across the globe available to support you in your
journey to *Inspire Self, Inspire Others, and Inspire the
World.*

---

www.secretan.com

INDEX